Get set to cook

CW01660293

Disclaimer

The information in this guide has been developed for guidance and best practice purposes.

Whilst every effort has been taken to ensure that the information provided in this guide is accurate and up-to-date at the time of printing, PACEY will not be held responsible for any loss, damage or inconvenience caused as a result of any inaccuracy, error or omission.

We refer to "parents" in this guide. Under Section 576 of the Education Act 1996, the term "parent" includes any person who is not a parent of the child, but has parental responsibility or who cares for him or her. According to the Children Act 1989, "parental responsibility" means "all the rights, duties, powers, responsibilities and authority which by law a parent of a child has in relation to the child and his property".

This nutrition guide has been reviewed by the Children's Food Trust to ensure that it is in line with the Voluntary Guidelines for Food and Drink in Early Years Settings in England.

The guide is also in line with best practice in Wales.

CHILDREN'S FOOD TRUST
Eat Better Do Better

Recipes in this guide are provided by the Children's Food Trust and further recipes suitable for 1- to 5-year-olds are available to download free of charge at **www.childrensfoodtrust.org.uk/eatbetterstartbetter**

Written by: Mel Parks and Pauline Phillips
Editors: Michelle Tempest and Ruth Bourne, PACEY
Publications Officer: Laura Coleman, PACEY
Designed by: Andy Bone, Synergy Group
Printed by: synergygroup.uk.com
Published by: PACEY Commercial Services Limited

ISBN 978-0-9929520-7-5

© Professional Association for Childcare and Early Years 2015

Tel: 0300 003 0005
Email: info@pacey.org.uk
Web: www.pacey.org.uk
PACEY Local: local.pacey.org.uk
@PACEYchildcare
www.facebook.com/paceylocal
PACEY Registered Charity No: 295981
PACEY Limited Company No: 02060964
PACEY Commercial Services Limited Company No: 02875417

Code COOK1 v06/15

pacey
professional association for childcare and early years

Contents

About PACEY ... 5
Supporting children's nutrition ... 6
Healthy eating in the early years ... 8
- Supporting children's health ... 9
- Balanced and nutritious diets ... 10
- A healthy start to the day ... 12
- Foods to limit ... 14

Inspiring children ... 18
- Experiencing food across the day ... 19
- Growing and cooking food together 21
- Enjoying the outdoors ... 24
- Exploring where food comes from .. 25

Tasty treats ... 27
- Keeping energy levels up ... 28
- Snack ideas for early years settings ... 30
- Getting the right balance ... 31

Exploring new tastes ... 34
- Supporting babies' emerging skills . 35
- Food fun and exploration ... 36
- Developing healthy eating habits ... 37
- Selective eaters ... 38

Catering for all children ... 40
- Time to celebrate ... 41
- Food customs of cultures and religions ... 43
- Vegan and vegetarian diets ... 45

Allergies and health conditions ... 46
- Food allergies ... 47
- Allergen guidance for childcare professionals ... 49
- Ways to manage allergies in a childcare setting ... 52
- Health conditions ... 55
- Intolerances ... 56

Keep it clean ... 57
- Getting food ready ... 58
- Storing food safely ... 59

Allergen FAQs ... 60
Early years recipes from the Children's Food Trust ... 61
- About the recipes ... 62
- Exploring new tastes: savoury main dishes ... 64
- Catering for all children: vegetarian main dishes ... 73
- Well balanced treats: puddings ... 80

PACEY resources ... 87
Further reading ... 88

About PACEY

PACEY is the Professional Association for Childcare and Early Years. Formed in 1977, we are a not-for-profit professional association with the purpose of supporting childcare professionals to deliver high standards of care and learning for children. Our members – childcare professionals across the sector – benefit from access to a wide range of expert support and resources. PACEY membership isn't just about what members receive on paper or online. It's about being part of a vibrant community of dedicated childcare professionals, delivering excellent standards, and together improving outcomes for children.

So, if you're not already a member of PACEY, visit us at **www.pacey.org.uk** to join.

As a member of PACEY, you make a commitment to your professionalism and the quality of childcare that you provide.

PACEY members sign up to a code of ethics and set of Professional Standards, helping to demonstrate an ongoing commitment to their career, to meet and exceed the expectations of their regulating authority and to provide the highest standards of care and learning for children.

pacey
professional association for childcare and early years

Supporting children's nutrition

This guide has been developed to help childcare professionals to support children's healthy eating by providing a balanced and nutritious diet. It also provides information and guidance to support you to understand and meet the allergen regulations in line with EU Food Information for Consumers Regulation which became law in 2014.

Childcare professionals play a key role in supporting children to develop healthy eating habits and work in partnership with parents to provide a balanced diet for children.

Throughout the guide, PACEY members have shared their valuable experiences and top tips, from tackling fussy eating to growing food with the children in their care. We have also provided helpful insights as to how each section relates to the Early Years Foundation Stage (EYFS) in England and the Foundation Phase or National Minimum Standards (NMS) for Regulated Childcare in Wales.

For more information on allergen regulations, visit: **www.food.gov.uk/business-industry/allergy-guide/allergen-resources**

The Children's Food Trust

The good practice advice throughout this guide has been reviewed by the Children's Food Trust to ensure that it is in line with the Voluntary Guidelines for Food and Drink in Early Years Settings in England.

The Children's Food Trust is the national charity championing every child's right to eat better, and so do better. The Trust is on a mission to help every child eat well – at school, at home and beyond. It worked with the early years and health sectors to develop national best practice guidance the Voluntary Food and Drink Guidelines for Early Years Settings in England and the Eat Better, Start Better programme, which helps early years providers to meet children's nutritional needs more consistently, and supports families with young children to develop the cooking skills and confidence they need to cook and eat more healthily.

Dr Patricia Mucavele is the Trust's Head of Nutrition. Her goal is to ensure everyone involved in early years food provision uses evidence-based nutrition advice as outlined in the Voluntary Food and Drink Guidelines for Early Years Settings in England.

For more information visit: **www.childrensfoodtrust.org.uk/eatbetterstartbetter**

Children under 12 months old

In the first 12 months of life, babies' nutritional requirements differ from those of children aged over one year. Detailed guidance on how to provide food and drink for those under one is not included within this guide. For more information on providing healthy food and drink to children from birth up to 12 months, please see the following resources:

The Department of Health's birth to five:
www.nhs.uk/planners/birthtofive/Pages/Birthtofivehome.aspx

Start4Life campaign:
www.nhs.uk/start4life

Caroline Walker Trust practical guide, Eating Well in the First Year of Life:
www.cwt-chew.org.uk/Pages/0-1.htm

First steps nutrition:
www.firststepsnutrition.org/newpages/Early_Years/eating_well-early_years.html

Healthy eating in the early years

- Supporting children's health
- Balanced and nutritious diets
- A healthy start to the day
- Foods to limit

Supporting children's health

It's no secret that good habits can be started early. A combination of eating regular healthy meals and snacks, and being active can reduce the risk of obesity, heart disease, diabetes, stroke and cancers, so children are more likely to live longer and healthier lives.

Childcare professionals play a key role in supporting children to develop healthy eating habits and work in partnership with parents to provide a balanced diet for children. It is reassuring for parents to know that their children are eating balanced meals when in childcare and at school, as well as at home.

Every childcare setting is different – you may provide some or all of a child's meals for the day, as well as snacks. It is important to be aware of your responsibilities around nutrition and healthy eating under the Early Years Foundation Stage (EYFS) in England and the Foundation Phase in Wales.

EYFS and Foundation Phase

Healthy eating is an integral part of the EYFS requirements in England and the National Minimum Standards for Regulated Childcare in Wales.

The EYFS Safeguarding and Welfare Requirements state: **"Where children are provided with meals, snacks and drinks, they must be healthy, balanced and nutritious. Before a child is admitted to the setting the provider must also obtain information about any special dietary requirements, preferences and food allergies that the child has, and any special health requirements."**

The EYFS and the Foundation Phase emphasise the importance for children to be are given opportunities to develop their skills, knowledge and understanding of how to keep their bodies healthy and safe, including through a healthy diet and physical exercise.

In England and in Wales, meals, snacks and drinks must be "healthy, balanced and nutritious" (EYFS p26). According to the National Minimum Standards for Regulated Childcare in Wales, any meals or snacks provided for children must also be "appropriate in quantity following recommendations in Welsh Government Food and Health Guidelines for Early Years and Childcare Settings (2009)" (NMS p30).

Whether in England or Wales, all childcare professionals must provide fresh drinking water. According to the EYFS in England, fresh drinking water must be freely available and accessible. Think about how the children in your setting would get some water if they wanted to without asking you.

In Wales, if parents are providing packed lunches they need to be informed of what can be stored safely (NMS, 12.6). This is good practice in England too. The National Minimum Standards for Regulated Childcare (Wales)also state that meals should be arranged to provide sociable opportunities for children, "using tables, seating and appropriate crockery and cutlery" (12.8).

Balanced and nutritious diets

The terms "balanced" and "nutritious" mean similar things for children and adults alike. However, children under 5 need less fibre (it can be too filling and leave less room for the other foods their bodies require) and more fat than older children and adults (for energy – though steer clear of too many saturated fats). Serving a variety of foods enables children to widen their tastes and explore different textures and combinations, and supports them in developing healthy eating habits to ensure they get all the nutrients they need.

Turn to page 36 to find out more about exploring different tastes and turn to page 14 to find out more about reducing saturated fats, sugar and salt in children's diets.

A balanced diet for children will include regular servings of:

Fruit and vegetables:

five portions a day are recommended (a portion being a child's handful).

Good for... carotenes (a form of vitamin A), vitamin C, zinc, iron and fibre.

Starchy carbohydrates:

such as potatoes, rice, pasta and bread (though limit the amount of wholegrain options – these are healthy, but filling, so too much could mean children don't have room for other nutritious foods).

Good for... energy, B vitamins, iron (if fortified) and fibre.

Milk and other dairy foods:

cow's milk can be introduced from 12 months old, and children over the age of 2 can start to switch from full-fat to semi-skimmed milk and lower-fat dairy products if they eat a varied diet. Skimmed milk is not suitable for under-5s as it contains lower amounts of calories and vitamin A.

Good for... calcium, protein, vitamin A, vitamin B-12 and potassium.

Meat, fish, eggs, beans and other non-dairy sources of protein:

such as meat (preferably lean), poultry, fish, eggs, beans, chickpeas, lentils, soya, tofu and textured vegetable protein.

Good for... protein, iron, zinc, omega 3 fatty acids and vitamins A and D.

Portion sizes

To read about portion size guidance for each of the four food groups see section 3 of the Children's Food Trust Voluntary Food and Drink Guidelines for Early Years Settings in England:

www.childrensfoodtrust.org.uk/ eatbetterstartbetter

Childcare professionals in Wales can also view section 3 of the Food and Health Guidelines for Early Years and Childcare Settings in Wales:

gov.wales/docs/phhs/publications/ foodandhealth/ 090414guidelinesen.pdf

Types of milk

Avoid skimmed milk and skimmed milk products, as these are low in fat and do not provide enough energy for children under the age of 5.

Goats' and sheep's milk can be provided for children over 12 months old. Unsweetened calcium fortified soya milk can be used as a non-dairy alternative to cows' milk for children aged over 12 months, and can be given as a main drink from 2 years.

Children under 5 years old should not be given rice milk as it has been found to contain small amounts of arsenic.

For this, and further information, see page 22 of the Voluntary Food and Drink Guidelines for Early Years Settings in England: **www.childrensfoodtrust.org.uk/eatbetterstartbetter**

Childcare professionals in Wales can also view section 6 and 12.11 of the Food and Health Guidelines for Early Years and Childcare Settings in Wales: **gov.wales/docs/phhs/publications/foodandhealth/090414guidelines en.pdf**

A healthy start to the day

Of the three main meals in a day, breakfast in particular can sometimes seem a rushed experience. Providing a healthy breakfast for children not only gives them the right sort of energy they need to start the day; eating breakfast with the children provides opportunities to talk about how our bodies need nutritious food in order to be healthy and work properly.

Some parents will provide breakfast for their children before they drop them off at their childcare setting. It is important to work in partnership with parents to make sure that the children always eat breakfast, whether at home or when they arrive at your setting. If you do provide breakfast for children, offer nutritious options such as porridge or muesli, fruit and toast; perhaps alternating with other favourites such as eggs, savoury bagels and cream cheese, or toasted teacakes with fruit toppings.

Be sure to notify parents about breakfast options and the allergens that may be present such as nuts, eggs, milk and cereals.

The Children's Food Trust offers plenty of breakfast menu ideas for early years settings in their seasonal menus. Visit: **www.childrensfoodtrust.org.uk/eatbetterstartbetter**

Breakfast in the setting

Breakfast is provided at Manor House Nursery for all children within their session price and has been seen as fundamental since the nursery opened in 2008. A healthy breakfast sets children up for the day and provides the energy and fuel so essential for young children's health, growth, development and wellbeing. Food must be seen not simply as the fuel for active bodies but it must be remembered that it supplies essential vitamins, minerals and fatty acids that maintain, repair and build young bodies and brains.

Breakfast offers a perfect opportunity for children to gather socially and develop independence; choosing from the various options available and in many cases serving themselves. Members of staff are on hand to toast the bread, cook the porridge or eggs as necessary, but are also encouraged to sit down and enjoy breakfast with the children. Small jugs allow children to pour out their own juice or milk and the dining rooms are designed to allow small group interactions.

Breakfast options vary but include:

- Cereals without added sugar – corn flakes, rice crispies, Weetabix, served with full-fat or semi-skimmed milk
- Fruit, fresh and dried
- Fruit juice, orange and apple
- Toast – white, brown and seeded
- Porridge in the colder months
- Boiled or scrambled eggs
- Low salt varieties of crumpets / muffins.

Clair Stevens, Manor House Nursery

Handy tip for providing fruit juice

Provide fruit juice at meal times only and dilute it (half juice, half water) as it contains sugars and acids that may damage children's teeth.

For further advice on the types of drinks to provide see page 22 of the Voluntary Food and Drink Guidelines for Early Years Settings in England:
www.childrensfoodtrust.org.uk/eatbetterstartbetter

Childcare professionals in Wales can also view page 14 of the Food and Health Guidelines for Early Years and Childcare Settings in Wales:
gov.wales/docs/phhs/publications/foodandhealth/090414guidelinesen.pdf

Foods to limit

There are three nutrients in food to limit when putting together a balanced menu: saturated fat, sugar and salt.

Increased consumption of foods which are high in saturated fat, salt and added sugars, low in essential nutrients, along with lower levels of physical exercise, are contributing to children becoming overweight or obese. According to the World Health Organisation, "Childhood obesity is one of the most serious public health challenges of the 21st century". According to the National Child Measurement Programme, the UK has one of the highest rates of childhood obesity in Europe, affecting more than a fifth of 4- to 5-year-olds and a third of 10- to 11-year-olds. Researchers at King's College London have recently suggested that childhood obesity in the UK may now be stabilising. However, the need remains for all of us to make a combined effort to support children's health and wellbeing and to be mindful of the effects of too much sugar and saturated fats.

How much fat, salt and sugar there is in meals and snacks depends on the amount of fat, sugar and salt found naturally in food and any added to food during preparation and cooking. It's good practice to cook from scratch whenever possible, as many prepared, manufactured foods can be high in fat, salt and sugar which can lead to an unbalanced, unhealthy diet.

Avoid high levels of saturated fat

Be careful that foods don't contain too much saturated fat. A diet high in saturated fat can, over time, raise the level of cholesterol in the blood and increase the risk of coronary heart disease, diabetes, and some cancers. This is why it is best to limit the amount of saturated fat that children eat, and provide some fat as unsaturated fats instead. Although a large study funded by the British Heart Foundation, Medical Research Council and Cambridge National Institute for Health Research Biomedical Research Centre last year found the link between saturated fat and heart disease does not appear to be as direct as previously thought, the NHS advises that more research is needed and guidelines on cutting down consumption of saturated fat in favour of unsaturated fats still stand.

How does saturated fat differ from other fats?

Fat is a concentrated source of energy (calories). Saturated fat is found in butter, pastries, cakes, biscuits and meat such as bacon, and meat products such as sausages. When you do a food shop, check the labels to see how much saturated fat is included in the food you buy.

Read the nutrition information on the food label to find out how much saturated fat is in the food. Remember, "saturates" and "saturated fat" mean the same thing. Lower saturated fat means lower risk of cardiovascular disease. Foods that are low in saturated fats contain 1.5g of saturates or less per 100g.

Some fat in the diet is important to ensure that young children get all the energy and nutrients they need to grow and be active:

- Vitamins A, D and E, which are important for growth, a healthy immune system, and healthy bones and teeth
- Essential fatty acids (including omega 3 fatty acids found in oily fish), which our bodies cannot make, and are needed for the development of our brains and other tissues

Do not add salt

There are clear guidelines about how much salt children should consume. The daily maximum amounts are:

- Less than 1g (infants up to 6 months)
- 1g (children aged 7-12 months)
- 2g (children aged 1–3 years)
- 3g (children aged 4–6 years)

Everyone needs a small amount of salt in their bodies in order to maintain fluid balance and to aid nerve and muscle function, but too much salt can lead to high blood pressure in adulthood, associated with heart disease, kidney problems and stroke. Always check any bought foods for added salt, and never add salt to food you are preparing for children.

When choosing bought foods, such as bread and bread products, crackers, and meat products. Check food labels and choose foods that are low in salt where possible (containing less than 0.3g salt per 100g).

For more advice on limiting salt in children's diets see page 28 of the Children's Food Trust Voluntary Food and Drink Guidelines for Early Years Settings in England: **www.childrensfoodtrust.org.uk/eatbetterstartbetter**

How to limit sugars

Children don't need to eat lots of sugary foods to consume the calories they need for their growing bodies. According to Public Health England, a 2012 survey showed tooth decay affects more than a quarter of 5-year-olds. Type 2 diabetes (usually adult-onset) is starting to be diagnosed in children in the UK and globally; one of the main risk factors is excess weight.

The National Diet and Nutrition Survey, published in May 2014, highlights that children in all age ranges are consuming too many non-milk extrinsic sugars (NMES) (also known as "added sugars"), too much salt and not enough fruit, vegetables and fibre.

In Wales, Public Health Wales worked with Cardiff University to produce the Picture of Oral Health report focusing on the oral health of 3-year-olds across Wales. To find out more, visit: **www.cardiff.ac.uk/_data/assets/pdf_file/0011/86546/First-report-for-WG-3yo-survey-2013-14v3.pdf**

Limiting the amount of sugary foods and drinks in children's diets, and how often they have them, reduces their risk of tooth decay. The sugar in fresh fruit and milk is not as damaging to children's teeth as the sugar in foods such as sweets, cakes, chocolate, fizzy drinks and added sugar and honey.

Limit children's sugar intake by avoiding sweet foods and drinks other than water and milk between meals. Check food labels and choose foods that are low in sugar where possible (containing less than 5g sugar per 100g).

HUG ME

Sources and resources

Change4Life:
www.nhs.uk/change4life/Pages/change-for-life.aspx

Children's Food Trust, Voluntary Food and Drink Guidelines for Early Years Settings in England – A Practical Guide:
www.childrensfoodtrust.org.uk/eatbetterstartbetter

Chowdry R, Warnakula S, Kunutsor S et al. Association of Dietary, Circulating, and Supplement Fatty Acids with Coronary Risk: A Systematic Review and Meta-analysis. See the NHS Response to this at:
www.nhs.uk/news/2014/03March/Pages/Saturated-fats-and-heart-disease-link-unproven.aspx

Department of Health (2011) Start active, stay active: A report on physical activity from the four home countries' Chief Medical Officers:
www.dh.gov.uk/en/Publicationsandstatistics/Publications/PublicationsPolicyAndGuidance/DH_127931

Marmot review of health inequalities (2010): Fair society, healthy lives. The report highlights that support in the early years is key in reducing these inequalities over a lifetime:
www.instituteofhealthequity.org/projects/fair-society-healthy-lives-the-marmot-review

National Child Measurement Programme (NCMP) England, 2013 – 14 school year published 3 December 2014:
www.hscic.gov.uk/catalogue/PUB16070

National Dental Epidemiology Programme for England, oral health survey of 5-year-old children 2012:
www.gov.uk/government/news/survey-finds-27-of-5-year-olds-have-tooth-decay

The National Diet and Nutrition Survey:
www.gov.uk/government/statistics/national-diet-and-nutrition-survey-results-from-years-1-to-4-combined-of-the-rolling-programme-for-2008-and-2009-to-2011-and-2012

NHS LiveWell:
www.nhs.uk/Livewell/childhealth6-15/Pages/Get-children-involved-inbeing-healthy.aspx

www.nhs.uk/Livewell/5ADAY/Pages/Portionsizes.aspx

www.nhs.uk/Livewell/Goodfood/Pages/salt.aspx

www.nhs.uk/Livewell/Goodfood/Pages/Fat.aspx

NHS:
www.nhs.uk/news/2015/01January/Pages/Child-obesity-rates-are-stabilising.aspx

www.nhs.uk/conditions/diabetes-type2/Pages/Causes.aspx

Public Health England (2014) Dental public health epidemiology programme oral health survey of three-year-old children 2013. A report on the prevalence and severity of dental decay:
www.nwph.net/dentalhealth/reports/DPHEP%20for%20England%20OH%20Survey%203yr%202013%20Report.pdf

Public Health England:
www.noo.org.uk/NOO_about_obesity/child_obesity

www.nwph.net/dentalhealth/survey-results5.aspx?id=1

Public Health Wales and Cardiff University (2014) Picture of oral health dental epidemiological survey of three-year-olds in Wales 2013:
www.cardiff.ac.uk/__data/assets/pdf-file/0011/86546/First-report-for-WG-3yo-survey-2013-14v3.pdf

Statutory Instrument 2014 No. 1603 The Requirements for School Food Regulations 2014):
www.legislation.gov.uk/uksi/2014/1603/pdfs/uksi_20141603_en.pdf

Welsh Government, Food and Health Guidelines for Early Years and Childcare Settings in Wales:
gov.wales/docs/phhs/publications/foodandhealth/090414guidelinesen.pdf

World Health Organisation:
www.who.int/dietphysicalactivity/childhood_why/en/

Inspiring children

- Experiencing food across the day
- Growing and cooking food together
- Enjoying the outdoors
- Exploring where food comes from

Experiencing food across the day

> “Rather than children hearing ‘Don’t touch that, don’t eat that’, while they’re cooking food with you, they want to be able to try it. It’s part of the fun – tasting bits, and exploring the feel and smell of the food. The result of the cooking isn’t as important as the taking part.”
>
> **Gabriela, childminder**

There is so much more to food than just the eating. Involving children in the food “journey” from produce to plate helps them to understand this and fosters a healthy attitude to food from a young age. Food also provides a great opportunity to support children’s everyday learning and development in a variety of ways. Turn to page 21 to find out how involving children in growing and preparing food can support their learning and development under the EYFS in England and Foundation Phase in Wales.

Preparing, cooking and eating food is an integral part of the day’s routine, and being relaxed in your approach to food will help children relax and have fun exploring it with you. Children can supply ideas for menus and help you shop for ingredients, gather fresh produce and help with the cooking.

You could also provide fresh vegetables and fruit in your role play area – including some more unusual produce that children may not be familiar with.

Make sure food stays contained in one area, and if children are eating that they wash their hands before doing so. Remember to complete a risk assessment before beginning an activity such as this. Fruit can also be included in treasure baskets for younger children to explore. This enables children to experience foods at their own pace, away from the potential pressure of the dining table (and then potentially be more likely to eat them at meal times). Consider children’s allergies when using food in activities and role play areas. Even if the food is not going to be consumed, some children may have a reaction to touching certain foods.

Pick 'n' mix lunch

I have been a registered childminder for 24 years and I enjoy supporting the children to eat healthily and learn about a balanced diet. I have a small vegetable plot in my garden and grow strawberries, raspberries, beans and salad items. I also take the children to pick-your-own farms which they love going to.

I like to offer children a choice of food to encourage them to try new things and to help all of them feel included in the meal. One activity based on having an element of choice is my special picnic, which can also be done at home:

1. Gather plastic boxes if you're going to take the food outside, or small bowls if you're staying in.
2. Empty the contents of your fridge to find titbits of food that can be eaten cold. For example, sweetcorn, carrot, cucumber, tomatoes, lettuce, cheese, ham, grapes, blueberries and strawberries.
3. Encourage the children to carefully help cut up the cucumber into bite-size pieces. They can also grate cheese and carrots. Or use kitchen scissors to cut ham and lettuce leaves.
4. Sort the ingredients into bowls or boxes – this is an ideal task for the children who aren't ready to use a knife or grater. Talk about the colour and texture of food as you're doing it.
5. Warm some pitta pockets or tortilla wraps (or pack cold for a picnic), and lay everything out on plates on a table or blanket.
6. Allow children to help themselves, talking to them about making sure there's enough for everybody. Also, talk to them about the different food groups that are represented, and how they can choose some food from each category.

With this activity, I've found that I can introduce more unusual food to the children such as radish or prawns and they are more likely to try them. It also makes everyone feel in control of what they are eating and included even if they don't like something or can't eat it.

Christine Emery, childminder

EYFS and Foundation Phase

Expressive arts and design (England)//Creative development (Wales)

Food is a brilliant medium for children to explore their imagination. Try making faces from chopped fruit and vegetables to make snack time fun.

Explore different colours and shapes of food – make a plate with all yellow food or all red food, or a plate of circles, and a plate of triangles. Food like cooked jelly and coloured spaghetti is great for messy play as it doesn't matter if babies and toddlers put their fingers in their mouths!

Remember that jelly is made from gelatine and so is unsuitable for vegetarians and some religious or cultural groups. See the table on page 44 of this guide, or page 50 of the Voluntary Food and Drink Guidelines for Early Years Settings in England: **www.childrensfoodtrust.org.uk/eatbetterstartbetter**

Childcare professionals in Wales can also view page 16 of the Food and Health Guidelines for Early Years and Childcare Settings in Wales: **gov.wales/docs/phhs/publications/foodandhealth/090414guidelinesen.pdf**

Growing and cooking food together

> "Dulcie has grown her own potatoes and other veg with her childminder and often helps to prepare the evening dinner. I think this helps to encourage her to eat more healthily as she's learning about where food comes from and how to prepare it."
>
> **Alana, mother to Dulcie and Hendrix**

Helping to grow food can be a big enticement for children to try the resulting produce. This can be as simple as herbs in a pot on the windowsill or putting bean sprouts in a clear jar so everyone can take turns watering them and easily see how they grow. Or if there's space outside, give each of the children their own spade (use plastic ones for younger children) and get planting! Use older children's love of team events and give the gardening activity a focus such as counting how many ripe tomatoes each team can pick. Remember to take photos to show to parents; this may encourage them too. As childminder Gabriela observed, "Many children don't grow things at home as their parents are busy, may think it's too expensive or may feel they don't have enough space."

For more information about growing food with children, see Growing Schools: **www.growingschools.org.uk** and the Royal Horticultural Society: **www.rhs.org.uk/children** or Health Challenge Wales: **www.healthchallengewales.org/gardening-with-schools**

Setting up an allotment

As a childminder and PACEY Local coordinator for Rushden, Northamptonshire, I wanted to set up a joint project to help children understand where their food comes from. Our garden is too small for growing and our dogs dig up anything we plant. So, the idea of a PACEY Local allotment was born. It has been enthusiastically taken up by two other childminders and we're hoping that more will join us on the journey as we get the plot established.

Here's how to set up an allotment or space for growing vegetables:

1. Ask the council or search online for a list of local allotment sites and put your name down on a waiting list. We had to wait three months for ours. Remember, you don't have to take the first site that is offered to you. Make sure it is convenient for you to be able to take children there often and in a good position (close to water taps, not too shady).
2. Prepare the soil. This can be hard work at an allotment which may not have been taken care of for a while. We got a group of adults together to clear weeds and dig the site over until it was ready for planting.
3. Involve the children in choosing seeds to plant. Take them to a garden centre or supermarket or flick through a seed catalogue at home. Talk about the food they like and what might be good to try.
4. Choose some unusual food to grow to keep it exciting. We've chosen cucamelon and blue and purple strawberries, as well as the usual favourites – potatoes, onions, leeks, carrots and cabbages. A must for any allotment is pumpkins for Halloween.
5. Plant the seeds with the children and encourage them to help with watering and monitoring how they grow.
6. Before planting out the allotment, include children's play areas in your plans. For example, a digging area and mud kitchen.
7. Risk assess your site. We've got a shed where we can keep adult and child-sized tools as well as a first-aid kit and hand-sanitising gel. We've also got a camping toilet and soon, we'll have a portable mobile sink for hand washing.
8. Check terms of your lease carefully. Some allotment areas prohibit sand pits or other play equipment and also restrict the size of sheds/buildings you can put on the allotment.

Finally, enjoy the fruits of your labour with fun tasting and cooking sessions. We always look forward to making tasty meals with fresh ingredients and exploring different jams and desserts. You could also try freezing, drying, bottling or pickling ingredients to preserve the food you have grown with the children.

Andrea Adams, childminder

EYFS and Foundation Phase

Mathematics (England) // Mathematical development (Wales)

Children can observe how many vegetables grow as well as the different shapes and sizes. Help the children to weigh the fresh produce and talk to them about which vegetables are the heaviest and which are lightest. You can also weigh and measure produce for recipes and serving portion sizes at mealtimes.

Understanding the world (England) // Knowledge and understanding of the world (Wales)

Growing fruit and vegetables helps children learn about where food comes from, about life cycles and how to look after plants. Understanding how mixing different ingredients together can make something completely new helps with knowledge of the world and how it works.

Personal, social and emotional development (England) // Personal and social development, well-being and cultural diversity (Wales)

Children feel a sense of accomplishment when they are eating food they have helped to grow and prepare – an excellent opportunity to develop self-esteem.

Communication and language (England) // Language, literacy and communication skills (Wales)

Food is a brilliant opportunity to use all the senses when talking about it – what does the food smell, look, feel, sound and taste like? Talk about the changes happening as it grows, or from raw to cooked. What does that soup sound like bubbling on the stove or the apple being chopped? Can you hear a banana being peeled?

Physical development (England & Wales)

Some children might be more developed in their fine motor skills so could help peel fruit and vegetables while others might find it easier to wash or mash ingredients, pour, stir or mix things with their hands.

For more information on learning about and through food, see page 53 of the Voluntary Food and Drink Guidelines for Early Years Settings in England:
www.childrensfoodtrust.org.uk/eatbetterstartbetter

or the Food and Fitness in the Curriculum in Wales publication:
learning.wales.gov. uk/docs/learningwales/publications/140626-food-and-fitness-in-the-curriculum-en.pdf

Food tasting activities are also valuable for teaching children about ingredients, the seasons and where food comes from, including food from different cultures. See page 53 of the Voluntary Food and Drink Guidelines for Early Years Settings in England:
www.childrensfoodtrust.org.uk/eatbetterstartbetter

Enjoying the outdoors

Forest school

One of the biggest changes that we notice when children start attending forest school sessions is their increase in appetite. The fresh air and increased physical experiences result in children who are eager to eat and will often enthusiastically try new foods. Every session includes a variety of fruit that children can access at any time and these are often taken by the children into dens and secret spaces to be eaten together. Lunch is provided as part of the session as it is in the nursery and is either cooked on the fire or using our outdoor oven. The experience in itself is much more sensory for the children and the smell, smoke and interest children show add to the social aspects of eating together. The children often help prepare lunch at the start of the session and the smell permeates through the woodland for the rest of the morning.

Favourites cooked on or around the fire include:

- Jacket potatoes cooked in foil and offered with a range of fillings such as cheese, tuna, baked beans or bolognese
- Corn on the cob cooked in foil
- Homemade vegetable soup prepared in the morning session by the children
- Wrap pizzas prepared by the children in the session using a variety of fillings
- Stir fry cooked in our large wok
- Toasted sandwiches
- Drop scones with fruit
- Baked fruit with cinnamon such as apples or bananas.

Clair Stevens, Manor House Nursery

EYFS and Foundation Phase

Communication and language (England) // Language, literacy and communication skills (Wales)

Children learn to follow instructions, particularly where safety is concerned, for example, not touching anything that is hot and keeping fingers out of the way when learning to peel vegetables or chop food (with a safety knife to begin with).

Personal, social and emotional development (England) // Personal and social development, well-being and cultural diversity (Wales)

Sharing, teamwork, making choices and cleaning up all support self-confidence.

Understanding the world (England) // Knowledge and understanding of the world (Wales)

Children can learn about how food cooks on the fire, why some ingredients melt and why some foods need to be cooked rather than eaten raw..

Physical development (England & Wales)

Preparing food can involve handling, chopping, mixing, pouring and kneading, which supports children's fine motor skills. Sitting together supports children to learn skills such as how to use cutlery and utensils, and helping themselves to food, pouring drinks and sharing.

Exploring where food comes from

Learning about where food comes from (plant or animal; from farms, gardens and allotments) appeals to children's natural curiosity and helps them to connect with food as a natural part of their lives and of the wider world. It supports the children in being able to make healthy choices for themselves as they get older. If it suits your practice, why not involve the children in planning your menus, too? This could help to give them an increased sense of confidence and encourage them to eat a varied diet.

The London Early Years Foundation (LEYF) runs over 30 community nurseries across London. Children from our nurseries regularly visit a farm which runs as both a working farm and a Trust offering free rural educational activities for groups, families and individuals, particularly children from disadvantaged urban areas. Activities include organic gardening, animal care, woodland craft, visiting beehives, a farm nature trail, pond dipping and outdoor cooking.

Children are involved in both the weekly planning meetings with staff and monthly meetings with nursery chefs. The meals they often request are dishes such as chicken casserole and macaroni cheese, rather than the potentially less healthy choices (for example, burgers and chips) that some parents think they may ask for.

We involve the children in themed activities, too. One nursery celebrated parsnips for a day: making soup, cake, painting with leftover parsnip pieces, and putting parsnip tops in water to grow roots. We also encourage healthy food habits for families through breakfast and picnic activities where parents join in and sessions on, for example, how to make soup or how to cook a balanced meal.

June O'Sullivan, Chief Executive, LEYF Nurseries

Sources and resources

British Nutrition Foundation:
www.foodafactoflife.org.uk/index.aspx

Children's Food Trust, Voluntary Food and Drink Guidelines for Early Years Settings in England – A Practical Guide:
www.childrensfoodtrust.org.uk/eatbetterstartbetter

Let's Get Cooking at Home:
letsgetcookingathome.org.uk/get-cooking/tips-cooking-kids

LEYF Nurseries:
www.leyf.org.uk/recipes-to-make-with-under-5s

NHS:
www.nhs.uk/livewell/goodfood/pages/kidsinkitchen.aspx

PACEY'S Cook and Learn video:
www.pacey.org.uk/mypacey/my_benefits/how-to_videos/cook__learn.aspx

PACEY's Cooking with Children factsheet:
www.pacey.org.uk/mypacey/my_benefits/factsheets/learning__development/cooking_with_children.aspx

Paddington Farm Trust:
www.paddingtonfarm.co.uk/

Welsh Government, Food and Health Guidelines for Early Years and Childcare Settings in Wales:
gov.wales/docs/phhs/publications/foodandhealth/090414guidelinesen.pdf

Welsh Government (2009) Food and Fitness in the curriculum in Wales:
learning.wales.gov.uk/docs/learningwales/publications/140626-food-and-fitness-in-the-curriculum-en.pdf

Tasty Treats

- Keeping energy levels up
- Snack ideas for early years settings
- Getting the right balance

Keeping energy levels up

Young children often have small stomachs so they need to eat little and often. Keeping them going all day means offering a regular supply of healthy snacks (two to three per day). Snack time can be a good opportunity to take a break, sit down and talk together, especially for those children that don't stay all day, and to make sure that the children take a drink of water to stay hydrated.

Childcare professionals must ensure that water is freely available to children at all times (EYFS in England, and National Minimum Standards for Regulated Childcare in Wales), but sometimes children get busy and forget to drink, so it is good to have a regular reminder.

Drinks other than water should be seen as part of the child's diet. For example, milk , fruit juices and smoothies all contain nutrients and calories. Smoothies in particular can be high in calories and so should be considered when calculating the children's overall intake. Like fruit juice, they also contain natural sugars which can cause dental decay.

Providing drinks

If you provide drinks other than milk and water for the children in your care, remember that fruit juices and smoothies should be limited to mealtimes only. Fruit juice and smoothies should be diluted (half juice, half water) as they contain sugars that may damage children's teeth.

For more information on the types of drinks to provide, see page 26 of the Voluntary Food and Drink Guidelines for Early Years Settings in England:
www.childrensfoodtrust.org.uk/eatbetterstartbetter

Childcare professionals in Wales can also view page 5 of the Food and Health Guidelines for Early Years and Childcare Settings in Wales:
gov.wales/docs/phhs/publications/foodandhealth/090414guidelinesen.pdf

Like drinks, snacks should be taken into consideration when thinking about a child's overall calorie intake and the range of food that they eat. They should be healthy, tasty and have nutritional benefit rather than just calories. Slices of fruit and raw vegetables are good snacks for children, for example carrot and celery sticks, apple chunks and orange wedges. Plain popcorn is also a good snack and avoids the main allergens as do rice crackers.

Remember that snacks such as oatcakes may contain gluten. Check snacks for any allergens and ensure that these are clearly communicated to parents.

Snack ideas for early years settings

- Mint and cucumber dip with cream crackers and kiwi
- Finger food selection of apple, banana and oatcake
- Mini English muffin toasted with vegetable fat spread
- Greek yoghurt with chopped fruit
- Melon and grape salad
- Banana with rice cakes
- Toasted bagel with strawberries
- Mini scotch pancakes/mini pancakes and milk
- Rice cakes and celery sticks filled with soft cheese
- Sugar snap peas with houmous
- Low salt variety crackers with soft cheese and sliced cherry tomatoes
- Plain popcorn (unsalted and unsweetened), grapes and pear slices
- Fruit snack: peach, nectarine, kiwi, apple and plum segments
- Sliced banana on toast
- Wholemeal pita served with houmous, cucumber and carrot sticks
- Kiwi fruit and milk
- Carrot sticks with pita bread and tsatziki
- Breadsticks, carrot and cucumber sticks and milk
- Finger food selection: carrot, cucumber and baby sweet corn with bread sticks and houmous
- Tuna pâté on wholemeal toast, sliced apple
- Crumpet toasted with low fat spread. Orange and grape salad
- Soldiers of toast, apple slices and thin Edam slices (Edam is lower in saturated fat than cheddar)
- Plain rice cakes with cottage cheese, apple and beetroot
- Fruit platter and milk
- Satsuma segments
- Fresh fruit salad and milk
- Oatcakes with cottage cheese, sliced apple
- Breadsticks with hard-boiled egg and tomato
- Mini scotch pancake with low fat spread and sliced strawberries

Collated and adapted from Caroline Walker Trust – eating well for under 5s in childcare and the Children's Food Trust's seasonal menus.

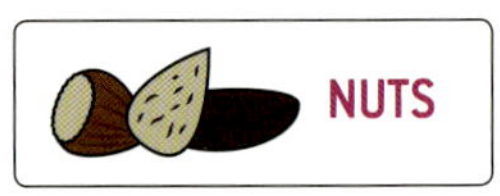

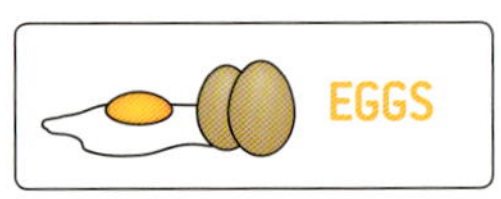

Getting the right balance

Some snacks contain high amounts of sugar, including many biscuits, cakes, children's yoghurts, dried fruit, sugary breakfast cereals and sweets. Avoid these foods between meals. Foods such as cereals with added sugar and sweets can be avoided altogether at your setting, whilst cooking cakes and biscuits from scratch allows you to lower the sugar content and incorporate fruit or vegetables such as carrots or beetroot. It also provides a fun learning activity for the children.

Avoid dried fruit at snack times

Provide dried fruit at meal times only rather than as a snack, as chewing dried fruit releases sugar which can stick to children's teeth and may damage children's teeth and lead to tooth decay. Dried fruit also often contains sulphites, which is one of the fourteen allergens to signpost in your setting.
For more information on how to limit sugar, see page 29 of the Voluntary Food and Drink Guidelines for Early Years Settings in England:
www.childrensfoodtrust.org.uk/eatbetterstartbetter

Childcare professionals in Wales can also view page 2 of the Food and Health Guidelines for Early Years and Childcare Settings in Wales:
gov.wales/docs/phhs/publications/foodandhealth/090414guidelinesen.pdf

In 2010, the Children's Food Trust collected evidence for the Advisory Panel on Nutrition in Early Years. Whilst fruit and vegetables are an essential part of children's diets, they found that some settings provided too much fruit and in cases where they provided only fruit for dessert the overall lunch provision didn't necessarily provide sufficient energy and variety to offer enough micronutrients (small amounts of essential vitamins and minerals) such as iron.

To find out more, see Laying the Table: Recommendations for food and nutrition guidance for early years setting in England. Available at: **www.childrensfoodtrust.org.uk/apfney**

Desserts, puddings and cakes made with cereals (such as rice or oats), milk and fruit can be included as part of a healthy, balanced diet for young children who are not allergic to gluten or dairy products. A healthy dessert should be provided as part of lunch and tea each day. Vary the desserts you offer with main meals each week.

Provide one dessert from each of the following groups each week to ensure children are getting a variety of different dessert types (offer alternatives for those with allergies):

- Hot fruit-based desserts such as crumbles or baked apples
- Milk-based desserts such as semolina
- Rice pudding or custard
- Yoghurt or fromage frais
- Cakes and biscuits containing fruit, such as carrot cake or fruit flapjack
- Cold desserts such as fruit salad

Desserts, puddings and cakes

Both bought and homemade cakes and biscuits should only be provided at mealtimes as the sugar in these can damage children's teeth. See page 24 of the Voluntary Food and Drink Guidelines for Early Years Settings in England: **www.childrensfoodtrust.org.uk/eatbetterstartbetter**

Childcare Professionals in Wales can also view page 5 of the Food and Health Guidelines for Early Years and Childcare Settings in Wales: **gov.wales/docs/phhs/publications/foodandhealth/090414guidelinesen.pdf**

EYFS and Foundation Phase

Personal, social and emotional development (England) // Personal and social development, well-being and cultural diversity (Wales)

Make snack and mealtimes a time when you all sit down together, taking a break from the work and activities of the day. It is a good time to develop social skills, taking turns in talking and helping each other. Children will learn how to share, work as a team, make choices, clean up, try new food and overcome dislikes. They will also develop an understanding that the right types of food and drinks are important for healthy bodies.

Sources and resources

Birth to five:
www.nhs.uk/planners/birthtofive/Pages/Birthtofivehome.aspx

The British Heart Foundation:
www.bhf.org.uk

Caroline Walker Trust (2011) Eating well: first year of life:
www.cwt.org.uk/wp-content/uploads/2014/07/CHEW-1stYearLifePracticalGuide.pdf

The Children's Food Trust's seasonal menus and recipes for early years settings:
www.childrensfoodtrust.org.uk/eatbetterstartbetter

Eating well for under-5s in childcare:
www.cwt.org.uk/wp-content/uploads/2014/07/Under5s.pdf

The Food Standards Agency:
www.food.gov.uk

First steps nutrition:
www.firststepsnutrition.org/newpages/Early_Years/eating_well-early_years.html

Start4life:
www.nhs.uk/start4life

Welsh Government, Food and Health Guidelines for Early Years and Childcare Settings in Wales:
gov.wales/docs/phhs/publications/foodandhealth/090414guidelinesen.pdf

Exploring new tastes

- Supporting babies' emerging skills
- Food fun and exploration
- Developing healthy eating habits
- Selective eaters

Supporting babies' emerging skills

Introducing a baby to solid foods, otherwise known as weaning, should start at around 6 months old. Moving onto solid foods is a major milestone in child development, and progress from there comes in leaps and bounds towards the time when children have settled into eating patterns and are used to a wide variety of foods. Learning to eat solid food is an important part of physical development as well as overlapping with communication and language, and personal, social and emotional development. Mealtimes are social occasions, too.

From around 6 to 8 months old, babies will usually be able to open their mouth for a spoon, move food around their mouths with their tongue, make chewing motions and hold finger foods. Offering finger foods helps babies learn to feed themselves and develop hand-to-mouth coordination to hold and use a spoon and bottle or cup. Weaning off bottles means children even without teeth, babies can make good headway with soft lumpy food and finger foods to chew on. Chewing helps to strengthen the jaw muscles, which in turn is important in learning to talk. By 12 to 18 months old babies can chew with their mouth closed, and children aged 2 to 3 years old are more adept at using a spoon and fork by themselves. Weaning off bottles means avoiding excessive sucking which in turn can affect tooth development. Using a cup also helps to develop talking.

Food related activities are great fun, sensory play for babies and young children, from feeling the texture of cooked spaghetti to helping to knead bread – all contributing to sensory experiences and the development of fine motor skills. You can easily adapt these activities to match the ages and abilities of children.

EYFS (England) and National Minimum Standards for Regulated Childcare Wales

Physical development (England & Wales)

Learning to drink from a cup, use utensils and cutlery, hold food, try new tastes and textures and chew food will all help with physical development.

There is also an element in physical development of making healthy choices which talking about food will help with, for example knowing the importance of a healthy diet and understanding where food comes from. Give children the chance to talk about what they like to eat while talking about healthy choices.

Digging in the garden, handling, mixing, pouring, kneading and chopping all support children's physical development. As does washing up. Make it easy for children to help with food preparation by giving them appropriate sized tools at the right level for them. Washing up can be made easier by giving them a bowl of soapy water at their height with a pile of clean tea towels.

Food fun and exploration

Many parents and childcare professionals will be familiar with the process of trial and error with children at mealtimes. Some children may refuse a food one day and yet eat it happily another day. Patience and persistence are key, along with not overwhelming children with too many options or too big a portion. Presenting a small selection of food on a plate or in the middle of a table and encouraging young children to feed themselves may be messy and often time-consuming, but it will reap rewards in the long run.

EYFS and Foundation Phase

Mathematics (England) // Mathematical development (Wales)

For older children, you could try putting numbers next to each plate of different food at snack time, showing the children exactly how many of each item the children are allowed to take. For example, five grapes, one piece of pitta bread, two chunks of cheese. This helps with portion control as well as number recognition and matching the figure with the amount.

Noughts and crosses

I have been nannying for seven years. Every family has a different way of living and has different dynamics which affects a child's personality and outlook. In the past I cared for a 3-year-old child who would refuse to eat most vegetables and meat. She was asking for fish fingers and chips, cakes and bread at mealtimes.

This concerned me and I tried to introduce her to lots of flavours, textures and ways to increase her interest in healthy foods, but nothing seemed to work effectively. The parents had been providing meals that their child requested.

At around this time I met Natasha Gavin, nutritionist and founder of 'I know why it's yum mum'. Attending her workshops gave me some new ideas and changed my approach to how to improve the child's diet. I started involving her in crafts that were fruit and vegetable themed, talked to her about how vegetables grow and why they are good for us, and took her to 'pick your own' farms. More often than not, the child had so much fun she did not realise she was eating something new. We made courgette cupcakes, kebabs, vegetable risottos and much more. Slowly the wheels turned and mealtimes weren't a struggle anymore.

Activity idea

Why not play a game of noughts and crosses with vegetables?

- Use breadsticks or cucumber strips to create the 'board'.
- Think of a variety of fruit and vegetables to make the 'noughts' and 'crosses'.
- Use some sweeter items at first, such as sweet potato to capture the children's attention.
- Later, swap out these sweeter items for other vegetables, such as radish.
- Mirror the play pieces you have used to the same foods on a plate to eat from. Keep the food and play separate.

Paula Vekoni, Nanny of the year 2013-2015

Developing healthy eating habits

You can support children to develop healthy eating habits through:

- Having regular meal and snack times
- Offering a variety of food
- Offering alternative snacks such as fruit or popcorn instead of sugary, fatty and salty snacks
- Offering water or milk (limiting fruit juices and smoothies to mealtimes only)
- Serving age-appropriate portions – children generally only eat until they're full, and can always ask for more if they want
- Sitting down together to eat in a relaxed environment, which enables children to learn through watching others
- Giving praise and encouragement for eating well and/or trying new foods
- Involving them in shopping for, preparing and cooking meals
- Partnership with parents to share what works and to ensure that children learn from consistent messages.

Selective eaters

> **"I try saying 'eat the food beginning with the letter…' so 'p' for peas and 's' for spaghetti. If we make it into a game they sometimes eat it even if they don't usually like it. Presenting the food in interesting ways also makes it more appealing."**
>
> **Vicki, mother to Arthur and Ted**

All of us have food preferences, and with young children this can present a challenge to parents or guardians and carers. There is a fine line between encouragement and pressure when it comes to mealtimes. Some children want to keep foods separate on their plates or eat one food item first before they start another. Others may be sensitive to a food's texture, smell, temperature or taste (so you could try serving it a different way), or be selective as a way of expressing their independence. Some don't like particular foods blended or mixed together.

Sometimes selecting certain foods masks an underlying issue, such as a child who has an allergy and fears having an allergic reaction to other foods. The important thing is to be patient and not force children to eat. Introduce just one new food at a time and keep offering a range of foods at each meal, including at least one item you know the child will like.

Some children with special educational needs and disabilities may be particularly selective with food. For example, children diagnosed with Autism Spectrum Disorder (ASD) may be sensitive to sensory experiences, such as how a food feels, and need additional support with trying new foods. They may also prefer that mealtimes are routine and predictable.

Supporting children with Autism Spectrum Disorder

I care for several children with special educational needs and disabilities (SEND), some of whom have Autism Spectrum Disorder (ASD). It's quite common for children diagnosed with ASD to have sensory issues with food and to be very selective with the food that they eat. I've found several strategies to help make meal times fun and relaxed.

Top tips for supporting children with ASD to eat varied foods:

1. I use picture exchange (PECS) cards. These are small, laminated photos of foods to support choice and to encourage and involve children. Seeing these pictures also prepares the children to know what we are going to eat, which helps to alleviate anxiety around food.

2. I work closely with parents to ensure that I follow any routines that encourage a child to eat. For example, peeling the skin from potato,
   or separating certain foods on the plate. Small things can sometimes make a big difference for the children.

3. A great way to encourage all children to eat different foods is to make meal times fun. I sometimes turn sandwiches into more interesting shapes with letter shape cutters, number cutters, animal cutters – whichever shapes you and the children choose. Remember to talk this through with ASD children before, however. They may prefer to make the shapes themselves from food that is presented as normal.

4. Add a teaspoon of the food that you'd like them to eat and build on it. Persevere, but without pressure; just make the food available for them to try. I went on one course and a nutritional expert said children need to refuse a food 30 times before it's a food they won't eat.

5. Make the most of helpful resources – I have found a very useful book: Can't Eat, Won't Eat – Dietary Difficulties and Autistic Spectrum Disorders. This book is excellent for all parents and professionals when supporting children who experience difficulties around food, eating and nutrition.

Ann Ross, childminder

Sources and resources

Baby Centre:
www.babycentre.co.uk/x552305/why-is-my-toddler-such-a-fussy-eater

Children's Food Trust, Voluntary Food and Drink Guidelines for Early Years Settings in England – A Practical Guide:
www.childrensfoodtrust.org.uk/eatbetterstartbetter

Change4Life:
www.nhs.uk/change4life/pages/healthy-eating-tips.aspx

Children's Food Trust online training course for early years professionals (part of the Children's Food Trust Learning Network), 'Encouraging young children to eat well':
www.childrensfoodtrust.org.uk/learningnetwork

Both PACEY's and The Children's Food Trust's online early years courses have been endorsed by the Council for Awards in Care, Health and Education (CACHE).

Early years outcomes (England):
www.gov.uk/government/publications/early-years-outcomes

EYFS Statutory Framework:
www.foundationyears.org.uk

Foundation Phase Framework:
gov.wales/topics/educationandskills/earlyyearshome/foundation-phase/?lang=en

Ten Steps for Healthy Toddlers:
www.infantandtoddlerforum.org/toddlers-to-preschool/little-peoples-plates/portion-sizes/

Catering for all children

- Time to celebrate
- Food customs of cultures and religions
- Vegan and vegetarian diets

Time to celebrate

As with all areas of your childcare practice, it is essential that all children feel represented and valued. A great way to do this is to share our experiences of food, and to introduce children to food from each other's cultures.

Discovering new foods

We use a favourite story to help introduce children to different fruits that they may not have come across before. It's called Handa's Surprise by Eileen Browne, and it's always a big hit. We read it especially in International Week, when we buy some of the more exotic fruits and try them together at nursery. In the story Handa, who lives in Kenya, chooses seven fruits to take to her friend in the next village as a treat – including guava, mango, pineapple and passion fruit. So we'll buy some of these, cut them up and try them as we read the story together. We also make a variety of dishes from around the world to share.

We encourage children to develop healthy lifestyles in other ways too. For instance, we have introduced mini sport lessons where a sports teacher comes in to train children on various skills. Children need their bodies to be able to function properly and respond so they can explore their environment, manipulate things and move effectively. Eating a range of nutritious foods and doing exercise help this to happen.

Top tips to encourage children to explore food:

1. Support children to eat with their peers (at nursery) and family (at home)
2. Present food so it's appealing to children's tastes
3. For celebrations or festivals involve children in preparing dishes from different countries
4. Use praise charts to encourage trying new foods.

Daksha Amin, Manager, Eveline Day Nursery, London

Plan ahead with the children for a special event – there'll be something that even the youngest child can participate in:

- Talk about why you'll be celebrating the event.
- There may be related activities you could do in the lead up to the event or on the day – such as stories, music, dancing, dressing up, arts and crafts, a play or show, an outing, or having someone come in to talk about what the event means to them and how they celebrate it.
- Discuss what food and drinks you might make and serve, including any of the children's ideas, and then choose together.
- Work out what decorations to have, including any special items to represent the event.
- Children may want to bring in toys or decorations from home to help create a special atmosphere.
- Remember to involve parents where possible.
- Older children can write invitations or share menus.

Here are some ideas to get your celebrations started:

- **Easter:** Spinach and egg mini pizzas; painted hard boiled eggs; carrot muffins; bunny shaped bread rolls

- **Christmas:** Star shaped cheese biscuits; cherry tomato, celery and carrot sticks mini Christmas 'trees' with dip; gingerbread people; Christmas tree decoration biscuits; reindeer carrot flapjacks

- **Diwali:** Baked onion bhajis; meat/chicken/chickpea curry; fruit and vegetable sticks with yoghurt dip; coconut balls; pineapple puddings

- **Chinese New Year:** Spring rolls; fried rice; honey or satay chicken sticks; mango pudding; baked bananas (a variation on fritters)

- **St David's Day:** Welsh rarebit toasts; chicken/ham and leek cheesy crumble; leek and cheese muffins; dragon shaped biscuits

Food customs of cultures and religions

It is important to cater for each individual child, and to work in partnership with parents to ensure that you follow a child's diet, which may be based on their culture or religious beliefs. Check with parents to understand clearly what foods to exclude or include for children, and whether some foods need to have been prepared in particular ways according to their beliefs and customs.

EYFS (England) and National Minimum Standards for Regulated Childcare in Wales

Food and drink requirements

The Statutory Framework for the EYFS section 3.47 states that "Before a child is admitted to the setting the provider must also obtain information about any special dietary requirements, preferences and food allergies that the child has, and any special health requirements. Providers must record and act on information from parents and carers about a child's dietary needs" (2014).

According to the National Minimum Standards for Regulated Childcare in Wales (Standard 12), the food and drink offered at a childcare setting should be varied and nutritious, and meet the religious, cultural and dietary requirements of each of the children.

EYFS and Foundation Phase

Understanding the world (England) // Knowledge and understanding of the world (Wales)

Trying food from different cultures and countries, using food to celebrate festivals and special occasions, and also exploring their own identity by talking about what they and their family eat all helps children understand the world in which they live.

Literacy (England)//Language, literacy and communication skills (Wales)

Many stories involve food and you can use these to help the children learn about ingredients, where food comes from and about food from different cultures. You'll notice that babies exploring food are often spreading it with their fingers and this is their first attempt at mark making. As children get older, they can start to recognise words, numbers and instructions in recipes.

Food customs of different religious and cultural groups

Food	Jewish	Hindu*	Sikh*	Muslim	Buddhist	Rastafarian**
Eggs	No blood spots	It varies	It varies	Yes	It varies	It varies
Milk/yoghurt	Not with meat	Yes	Yes	Yes	Yes	It varies
Cheese	Not with meat	It varies	It varies	It varies	Yes	It varies
Chicken	Kosher only	It varies	It varies	Halal only	No	It varies
Mutton/lamb	Kosher only	It varies	It varies	Halal only	No	It varies
Beef/beef products	Kosher only	No	No	Halal only	No	It varies
Pork/pork products	No	No	Rarely	No	No	No
Fish	Fish with fins & scales only	Fish with fins & scales only	It varies	It varies	It varies	Yes
Shellfish	No	It varies	It varies	It varies	No	No
Butter/ghee	Kosher only	It varies	It varies	It varies	No	It varies
Lard	No	No	No	No	No	No
Cereal foods	Yes	Yes	Yes	Yes	Yes	Yes
Nuts/pulses	Yes	Yes	Yes	Yes	Yes	Yes
Fruit and vegetables	Yes	Yes	Yes	Yes	Yes	Yes

"It varies" means that some people within a religious group would find these foods acceptable
* Strict Hindus and Sikhs will not eat eggs, meat, fish, and some fats.
** Some Rastafarians are vegan.

For more information about Kosher food: **www.koshercertification.org.uk/whatdoe**

For more information on Halal food: **halalfoodauthority.com/definition-of-halal**

Sourced from: **www.childrensfoodtrust.org.uk/assets/uifsm/special-diets**

Vegan and vegetarian diets

Some people choose to bring up their babies and children on a vegetarian or vegan diet. Lacto-ovo-vegetarians eat both dairy products and eggs; this is the most common type of vegetarian diet. Lacto-vegetarians eat dairy products but avoid eggs, and vegans do not eat dairy products, eggs, or any other products which come from animals.

Alternative sources of protein for vegetarians and vegans include: beans and pulses, soya, quinoa, tofu and nuts, although many childcare settings prefer to be nut-free because of the severity of nut allergies in some children. Talk to the parents to find out exactly which foods they are happy for you to give to their child, and what they eat at home.

Sources and resources

Children's Food Trust:
www.childrensfoodtrust.org.uk/uifsm/special-diets

First steps Nutrition Eating well:
vegan infants and under-5s:
www.firststepsnutrition.org/newpages/Early_Years/eating_well-early_years_vegans.html

Nutritional guidance for early years: food choices for children aged 1-5 years in early education and childcare settings (Scottish Executive), Appendix 5, Food for religious faiths and beliefs:
dera.ioe.ac.uk/8024/1/0021563.pdf

Allergies and health conditions

- Food allergies
- Allergen guidance for childcare professionals
- Ways to manage allergies in a childcare setting
- Health conditions
- Intolerances

Food allergies

Allergies are now a significant issue for children in the UK. According to Allergy UK, each year the number of people with allergies increases by five per cent, half of all affected being children.

Food allergies are more common in children who come from families where other members have allergies. Babies who have eczema are particularly at risk of developing food allergies.

A food allergy is an adverse immune response to specific proteins found in food, and even a tiny trace of a food can cause a reaction in someone who is allergic to it.

According to the EAT website (Enquiring About Intolerance), food allergy develops in approximately six per cent of children in the UK. Children are more likely to outgrow allergies to foods such as cow's milk and egg compared with peanuts and fish, which are more likely to be lifelong allergies.

EYFS (England) and National Minimum Standards for Regulated Childcare in Wales

As a childcare professional, you have a responsibility to think about the foods that you provide to the children and to follow each child's individual care plan.

The Early Years Foundation Stage (EYFS) safeguarding and welfare requirements state that providers of childcare for children from birth to 5 should have clear policies and procedures for safeguarding children. They should also "obtain information about any special dietary requirements, preferences and food allergies that a child has, and any special health requirements". It is good practice to include an allergen policy and have a procedure in place.

If you are a PACEY member, you can view sample policies, including a food and drink policy, at **www.pacey.org.uk**

Childcare providers must obtain, record and comply with information about children's dietary requirements, including cultural and religious requirements and "therapeutic diets for officially diagnosed food allergies". (NMS, Wales Standard 12/EYFS, England, 3.47, p26) In England, this information should be obtained before a child starts at the setting, and it should include any food preferences and any special health requirements. Also, providers "must record and act on information from parents and carers about a child's dietary needs".

Allergen guidance for childcare professionals

The Food Standards Agency has produced guidance to help all food providers, including early years and childcare providers to understand the new EU Food Information Consumer (FIC) regulation and meet their legal responsibilities to provide accurate allergen information.

Remember you are not being asked to list all the ingredients in the food you produce; you are being asked to document the allergens contained. As a childcare professional, you're already covering some of the requirements as you have to obtain allergen and intolerance information before a child starts at your setting.

Your responsibilities under the allergen regulations

The EU Food Information for Consumers Regulation came into effect in December 2014, which means that all early years settings now have a **legal responsibility** to provide accurate allergen information to parents, children and staff for every food and drink item you provide that contains any of the 14 allergens as ingredients. In practice this means you need to identify (with the help of your suppliers and/or by reading food labels) if any of your food and drink items (bought in and cooked from scratch) has any of 14 different allergens and then communicate this to parents, children and staff.

How to provide this information:

- **Written details** of the allergens should be listed clearly, for example for recipes and menus.
- Oral information on allergens must be able to be checked by others (**verifiable**), confirmed as accurate and the same information should be given every time (**consistent**).
- All staff must be aware of **policies and procedures** around handling and communicating allergen information.
- All staff should receive **training** on handling and effectively communicating allergen information.

For information on the EU Food Information for Consumers Regulation 1169/2011, visit **www.ec.europa.eu/food/food/labellingnutrition/foodlabelling/proposed_legislation_en.htm**

The main 14 allergens

There are 14 allergens that childcare professionals now need to display if they are being given as part of the food you provide at your setting. The list of 14 allergens (below) is not exhaustive – there may be other foods that the children in your care are allergic to. The list below represents the most common and potent allergens across the EU and these foods are responsible for the majority of the allergic reactions occurring within the food allergic population.

Celery – This includes celery stalks, leaves, seeds and the root called celeriac. You can find celery in celery salt, salads, some meat products, soups and stock cubes.

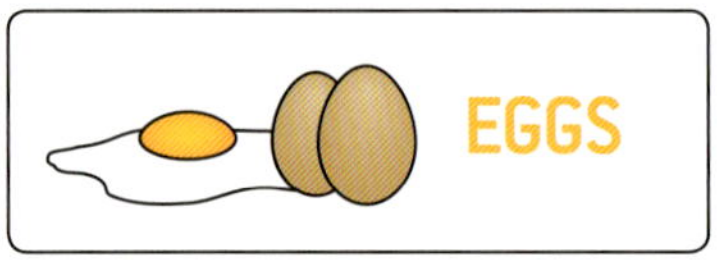

Eggs – Eggs are often found in cakes, some meat products, mayonnaise, mousses, pasta, quiche, sauces and pastries or foods brushed or glazed with egg.

Cereals containing gluten – Wheat (such as spelt and Khorasan wheat/Kamut), rye, barley and oats is often found in foods containing flour, such as some types of baking powder, batter, breadcrumbs, bread, cakes, couscous, meat products, pasta, pastry, sauces, soups and fried foods which are dusted with flour.

Peanuts – Peanuts are actually a legume and grow underground, which is why it's sometimes called a groundnut. Peanuts are often used as an ingredient in biscuits, cakes, curries, desserts, sauces (such as satay sauce), as well as in groundnut oil and peanut flour.

Crustaceans – Crabs, lobster, prawns and scampi are crustaceans. Shrimp paste, often used in Thai and south-east Asian curries or salads, is an ingredient to look out for.

Lupin – Yes, lupin is a flower, but it's also found in flour! Lupin flour and seeds can be used in some types of bread, pastries and even in pasta.

Milk – Milk is a common ingredient in butter, cheese, cream, milk powders and yoghurt. It can also be found in foods brushed or glazed with milk, and in powdered soups and sauces.

Molluscs – These include mussels, land snails, squid and whelks, but can also be commonly found in oyster sauce or as an ingredient in fish stews.

Mustard – Liquid mustard, mustard powder and mustard seeds fall into this category. This ingredient can also be found in breads, curries, marinades, meat products, salad dressings, sauces and soups.

Nuts – Not to be mistaken with peanuts (which are actually a legume and grow underground), this ingredient refers to nuts which grow on trees, like cashew nuts, almonds and hazelnuts. You can find nuts in breads, biscuits, crackers, desserts, nut powders (often used in Asian curries), stir-fried dishes, ice cream, marzipan (almond paste), nut oils and sauces.

Fish – You will find this in some fish sauces, pizzas, relishes, salad dressings, stock cubes and Worcestershire sauce.

Soya – Often found in bean curd, edamame beans, miso paste, textured soya protein, soya flour or tofu, soya is a staple ingredient in oriental food. It can also be found in desserts, ice cream, meat products, sauces and vegetarian products.

Sulphites – This is an ingredient often used in dried fruit such as raisins, dried apricots and prunes. You might also find it in meat products, soft drinks, vegetables as well as in wine and beer. If you have asthma, you have a higher risk of developing a reaction to sulphur dioxide (sulphites).

Ways to manage allergies in a childcare setting

Use the PACEY allergy stickers and menu plans to help share information with parents about the food you are providing with potential allergens.

Food providers can no longer say that a food "may contain" an allergen. You must state if food provided at your setting contains any of the 14 allergens listed.

Here are some suggestions for incorporating the allergen guidance in your setting:

- Use rolling menus, so that parents know what their child will eat on a given day.
- Tell parents about the regulations and signpost parents to "Advice on food allergen labelling" – an allergy leaflet for parents by the Food Standards Agency.
- Provide parents with accurate and consistent information about the food you're providing. This can be verbal information, but it is good practice to write it down as evidence that you are fulfilling the allergen requirements.
- Put information on display about each meal and snack that you provide, rather than giving parents information to take away.

Remember that information about allergens must be able to be checked by others (verifiable), confirmed as accurate and the information given should be consistent.

If a child has a diagnosed allergy, work with the parents to develop an allergy management plan. This should include:

- The child's details
- Information on foods the child can and cannot eat
- Emergency contact details for the parents or guardians
- Emergency procedure to use if an allergic reaction occurs
- Medication that the child can be given
- Staff training required
- Any precautionary measures that are needed (for example, for outings or special occasions. How you manage food in your setting risk assessments, cross-contamination)
- Review the diet on a regular basis.

(Source: Food and Health Guidelines, Welsh Assembly Government)

In larger group settings, you could try putting up photographs in the food preparation area of any children who have allergies. Add details of the food/s they are allergic to and where to find their management plan.

Some children with severe allergies wear wrist bands or badges so they are identifiable to anyone who has been trained. If you think that a child has a severe allergic reaction:

- Do not move them unless they are in immediate danger
- Administer any prescribed auto-injector device, if available
- Ring 999 and ask for an ambulance with a paramedic straight away
- Explain that the child could have anaphylaxis (pronounced 'anna-fill-axis')
- Send a responsible person outside to wait for the ambulance
- Contact the parent/guardian of the child after you have called an ambulance.

Top tips for allergens

I am a childminder and PACEY Associate and have taken care of many children with allergies. I work with my husband and we are very proud of our childminding setting's healthy eating gold award from our local authority, Kirklees Council.

Just before the allergen guidance came out in December 2014, we listed the allergens in the meals we provide for the children and updated our menus and recipes which is part of the information we give parents on induction.

All the children have a home-cooked evening meal with us, whether they come after school or they've been with us all day. We have about 12 recipes that we know all the children will eat, and we serve one of those each day being careful not to repeat the school lunch menu.

1. Keep an eye on ingredients. Even though we always cook the same food and know what is in each recipe, we know that even the same branded product can change, so we regularly check the food labels.
2. Prepare fresh food so that you know exactly what is in each meal.
3. Be careful with weaning babies. I work closely in partnership with parents when taking care of a weaning baby. I try not to give them anything containing the main listed allergens, for example, gluten or egg that the parents haven't tried first.
4. I prefer to provide food myself, as if all the children are eating food they have brought from home, it is easy for them to cross-contaminate by sharing things.
5. Make everyone the same food to eat, so the child with an allergy doesn't feel different. If someone isn't allowed toast because of the gluten, I would use the same gluten-free bread for everyone. I have a child who doesn't eat minced meat because of the texture so it no longer appears on the menu.
6. Be careful when at toddler groups or other people's houses. I cared for one toddler who required a dairy-free diet. She always knew that the food she was allowed had to come from my bag and she protested if anyone else offered her a biscuit from the main snack tray.
7. Keep a record of the food you give to the children, but make it easy for yourself. By sticking to the same 12 recipes, I can give parents the information on induction and I don't have to prepare new menus every week or fortnight.
8. Remember to check food items that you use in play. For example, play dough or gloop. Play dough can be made with rice flour instead of wheat flour containing gluten. It is a good idea to check any arts and crafts materials for allergens in the ingredients, for example some paints contain egg.
9. Research alternatives so that a child with allergies can still enjoy food activities with the other children, for example, baking. We found an egg-replacement powder that meant one child with a dairy-free diet could enjoy baking and eating buns.

Sue Asquith, childminder

Ongoing research into allergies

In February 2015, King's College London published the results of their LEAP (Learning Early About Peanut Allergy) study, led by Professor Gideon Lack. This is the first study to show that consumption can be an effective strategy to prevent food allergy. The study looked at a sample of children who were considered at high risk of developing peanut allergy. Half of the children were asked to eat food containing peanuts three or more times a week. The other half were asked to avoid eating peanuts until they reached 5 years old. The study showed an 80 per cent reduction in peanut allergy for those who consumed peanuts during the study.

Professor Lack added, "The study also excluded infants showing early strong signs of having already developed peanut allergy; the safety and effectiveness of early peanut consumption in this group remains unknown and requires further study. Parents of infants with eczema and/or egg allergy should consult with an allergist, paediatrician or their general practitioner prior to feeding them peanut products."

For further information on Professor Lack's study, visit:
www.kcl.ac.uk/newsevents/news/newsrecords/2015/February/Eating-peanut-at-an-early-age-prevents-peanut-allergy-in-high-risk-infants.aspx

Food Standards Agency Food allergy and intolerance research
www.food.gov.uk/science/research/allergy-research

Food Standards Agency Food allergy and intolerance, an overview of research and work **www.food.gov.uk/sites/default/files/multimedia/pdfs/publication/allergy_fsa_overview.pdf**

Health conditions

You may find that a child in your care has a specific health condition, rather than an allergy or an intolerance. Here are some examples of health conditions that can occur in children and affect their dietary needs:

Coeliac disease

Children with coeliac disease have a bad reaction in their bodies to gluten. This is an autoimmune condition where their body sees gluten as a threat and attacks it. This is different from a gluten intolerance. Children with coeliac disease must not be given gluten, which is a protein found in wheat, rye and barley. This means that food such as pasta, bread/toast, biscuits and cakes should not be given to children with coeliac disease unless they are made with gluten-free products.
For common signs and symptoms of coeliac disease, visit:
www.nhs.uk/Conditions/Coeliac-disease/Pages/Symptoms.aspx

Diabetes

This is a condition where not enough or no insulin is being produced by the body, which means it cannot properly regulate glucose. Diabetes in young children is a serious medical condition (Type 1) requiring daily testing of glucose levels in their blood and insulin injections. Children with Type 1 diabetes will have instructions on exactly when to have meals and snacks, and you will need to follow a parent's instructions carefully.

The majority of children with diabetes have Type 1, however, an increasing number are developing Type 2 diabetes. For more information, visit:
www.diabetes.org.uk/Guide-to-diabetes/Living_with_diabetes/Your-child-and-diabetes

Inflammatory bowel disease

The term inflammatory bowel disease (IBD) is used to describe ulcerative colitis, which affects the large intestine, and Crohn's disease, which can affect the entire digestive system. Although more common in teenagers and adults, IBD can occur in children.

For more information, visit:
www.nhs.uk/conditions/Inflammatory-bowel-disease
or **www.crohnsandcolitis.org.uk**

Intolerances

Food intolerance means that your body has difficulties processing a substance. It is not life-threatening. Food intolerance is more common than allergies, and the symptoms of food intolerance tend to start later, often hours after eating the problem food. Typical symptoms include bloating and stomach cramps. People with food intolerance may still be able to eat that food in small quantities, whereas allergy symptoms will happen immediately with even a small amount of the food.

Allergy symptoms will often appear as soon as the child has eaten the food for the first or second time. These could be: an itchy rash around the mouth, swelling of the face, runny nose and itchiness as well as vomiting.

See page 53 (above) to find out what to do if a child has a severe allergic reaction.

Resources and support

Allergy UK:
www.allergyuk.org

Children's Food Trust Voluntary Food and Drink Guidelines for Early Years Settings in England, page 48 Food allergies and food intolerances:
www.childrensfoodtrust.org.uk/eatbetterstartbetter/practicalguide

Coeliac UK:
www.coeliac.org.uk

Diabetes UK:
www.diabetes.org.uk

Food Standards Agency:
www.food.gov.uk

Food and Health Guidelines – For Early Years and Childcare Settings, Welsh Assembly Government (2009):
http://gov.wales/topics/health/improvement/index/guidelines/?lang=en

NHS:
www.nhs.uk/conditions/allergies

PACEY allergen resources, including sample menus and factsheets:
www.pacey.org.uk/mypacey

PACEY allergen stickers, to be used in conjunction with menu templates, journals and record cards:
shop.pacey.org.uk

Vegetarian Society:
www.vegsoc.org

Keep it clean

- Getting food ready
- Storing food safely

Getting food ready

Part of your job when preparing and cooking food is to practice good hygiene and share those habits with the children. It is also a requirement of the EYFS in England and the National Minimum Standards for Regulated Childcare in Wales. To read more about how food hygiene links with the EYFS and National Minimum Standards for Regulated Childcare in Wales, see the page opposite.

If you are newly registered in England and providing food, Ofsted automatically pass on your details to the local authority. Longer standing childminders who begin to provide food must register themselves with the local environmental health department. In Wales, all childcare and early years settings that regularly serve snacks or meals should register with the local environmental health department.

Each local environmental health department will have their own procedure. Some may inspect initially; some send a questionnaire to complete.

Food poisoning can make children seriously ill. The most serious types of food poisoning are due to bacteria. The more bacteria present, the more likely you are to become ill. The good news is that lots can be done to prevent illness, infection and the spread of bacteria by keeping things clean. If food poisoning occurs in your setting affecting two or more children, you must notify Ofsted or your childminder agency (England) or your local Health Protection Team, Environmental Health and CSSIW (Wales).

Getting food ready

- Wash hands before touching food
- Wash hands straightaway after touching raw meat, poultry and fish
- Wear a clean apron
- Cover any wounds or cuts with a coloured dressing
- Keep pets out of the way
- Think about cross-contamination – use separate (preferably colour-coded) chopping boards and utensils
- Make sure your equipment and work surfaces are clean
- Tie hair back and keep nails short
- Consider any allergies that children may have

Safer food, better business pack

For this, and further information about food safety, visit
www.food.gov.uk/business-industry/caterers/sfbb
and download the relevant Safer food, better business pack. The pack gives useful advice and contains helpful information about food safety, cooking, cleaning and caring for a child with a food allergy.

Storing food safely

Some settings only serve food that the parents have provided, but there is still a responsibility to make sure that food is stored safely and that parents are aware of food hygiene. Let parents know what food you can store safely at your setting and if you don't have room in your fridge to store the food, or you will be out and about, ask parents to think about using a cool bag to keep their child's food chilled.

Storing food safely

- Wrap and cover food.
- Check fridge and freezer temperatures regularly
- Store food correctly in the refrigerator, for example, using different shelves for storing different types of food, with raw meat kept separately at the bottom
- Check best before and use-by dates.
- Do not keep opened cans in the fridge but transfer to an airtight container
- Wash all fruit and vegetables
- If parents are providing food, including breast milk if a parent expresses for a baby in your care, ensure that you store this correctly.

Keeping it clean

The requirements for food hygiene and safe preparation for food go beyond the National Minimum Standards in Wales and the EYFS in England, as Food Standards Agency, Environmental Health (in Wales), and local authority (in England) guidelines also need to be followed. In Wales, the statement "all food is stored safely", (12.6) encompasses a childcare provider's duty. This is further outlined in the Infection Prevention and Control for Childcare Settings (Wales) 2014:
www.wales.nhs.uk

In England, the EYFS states that "there must be suitable facilities for the hygienic preparation food for children, if necessary, including suitable sterilisation equipment for babies' food" (EYFS 3.48).

Also, in England, "providers must be confident that those responsible for preparing and handling food are competent to do so. In group provision, all staff involved in preparing and handling food must receive training in food hygiene" (EYFS 3.48).

Notify Ofsted or your childminder agency of any food poisoning outbreak affecting two or more children cared for on the premises within 14 days. Childcare professionals in Wales should notify the local Health Protection Team, Environmental Health and CSSIW as soon as possible in the event of any outbreak of food poisoning.

Allergen FAQs

Q. If none of the children in my care have allergies do I still have to produce a list each day of the allergens present in food? Or is the requirement just for those providers who have children with allergies in their care?

A. PACEY recommends that the allergens are displayed in accordance with the regulations. This will ensure that if challenged, you are meeting the regulations. We have created the stickers and menu templates which could really help with this.

Q. If children bring food with them, do we still need to display the allergens?

A. Providing allergen information for parents' own food is not required. However, you must ensure that there is no mix up or cross-contamination during the serving or storing of the food that has been provided.

Q. I am a nanny – therefore in a parent's home – do the allergen guidelines apply to me?

A. As a nanny working in the parents' home, the parent will supply the food. Therefore, the food allergen guidance does not apply.

Q. If there is a cake sale anywhere, will the organisers need to provide the allergen information? For example, Macmillan charity bake sale days.

A. No, as the rules are not intended for one off sales. However, PACEY would recommend as best practice to provide this information if possible.

Q. If a parent wants to send cakes in with their child for their birthday (i.e. they are not purchased) do they need to provide the information?

A. If a child brings in a cake to share with the other children it would depend on two things:

1. The policy at the childminding setting, school or nursery
2. It would be advisable to provide information if the cake is to be shared so the practitioners can make sure they can meet safeguarding/duty of care obligations and not give the cake to a child with an egg allergy for example.

Option 2 is best practice in the eyes of the European Food Information Council (EU FIC), and fits in with the safeguarding agenda for childminders, schools and nurseries.

Q. Does the allergen guidance apply to activities that the child will be doing, such as messy play where they may be touching possible allergens or is it only what they are eating?

A. The new regulations apply to food only, including drink. However, if a child has known allergies then exposing them to an allergen even in a non-food form would possibly cause an allergic reaction (especially where hands are placed anywhere on the face). This duty of care is covered in the safeguarding and welfare requirements of the EYFS.

Q. How do bakeries and greengrocers with loose packaging display allergen information?

A. They can provide an upfront signpost to where to obtain the information or declare on a tent card, shelf barker (label that is on the shelf).

For a full list of allergen FAQs, PACEY members can visit **www.pacey.org.uk/mypacey**

Early years recipes from the Children's Food Trust

About the recipes

Exploring new tastes: savoury main dishes
Recipe 1: Mixed bean and root vegetable stew
Recipe 2: Lamb curry
Recipe 3: Beef and vegetable enchiladas
Recipe 4: Chicken risotto
Recipe 5: Fish pie with sweet potato

Catering for all children: vegetarian main dishes
Recipe 6: Potato and lentil cakes
Recipe 7: Chickpea and vegetable curry
Recipe 8: Quorn and vegetable couscous
Recipe 9: Savoury omelette
Recipe 10: Ratatouille and mozzarella

Well balanced treats: puddings
Recipe 11: Raspberry purée and fromage frais
Recipe 12: Cocoa and beetroot cake
Recipe 13: Warm winter salad
Recipe 14: Banana cinnamon rice pudding
Recipe 15: Crunchy summer crumble and yoghurt

About the recipes

The recipes in this section are from the Children's Food Trust spring/summer and autumn/winter menus and recipes for early years settings. Each recipe has been tried and tested by early years settings. The recipes reflect the best practice guidance and recommended typical portion sizes published in the Children's Food Trust Voluntary Food and Drink Guidelines for Early Years Settings in England. They also reflect best practice guidance in Wales.

For further information, please visit:
www.childrensfoodtrust.org.uk/eatbetterstartbetter and **gov.wales/topics/health/improvement/change**

Ingredients

The ingredients used in each recipe are in line with the food and drink guidelines and examples of good practice listed in the Children's Food Trust Voluntary Food and Drink Guidelines for Early Years Settings in England. Quantities of ingredients are given in both metric and household measures where appropriate. These have been given as a guide. Individual products, brands and food items may vary in weight from those given.

Number of servings per recipe

Most recipes include two sets of ingredient weights, to make either five or 20 servings. This means that the recipes can be used by childminders cooking for a small number of children, as well as nurseries, pre-schools and children's centres cooking for larger numbers of children. Where the quantities are more suited to 10 servings, those weights are given. The ingredient quantities in the recipes can be multiplied to cater for larger numbers of children where needed.

Typical portion sizes

The recipes include suggested portion sizes based on an average portion size for one to four-year-olds, so would be appropriate in a setting providing food and drink for a range of children. Portion sizes for 1- to 2-year-olds and 3- to 4-year-olds are also shown where appropriate. It is important to note that young children's appetites vary, and that they should be encouraged to eat healthy food according to their appetite. Typical portion sizes given are for the recipe as served.

Managing food allergies and intolerances

Food allergies or intolerances must be taken seriously. Early years settings and their caterers should work closely with parents to support children with medically verified allergies or intolerances and there should be a protocol in place. For more information on managing food allergies in early years settings visit the Allergy UK website.

Allergy information

The new EU and UK laws (The EU Food Information for Consumers Regulation enforced in the UK by the Food Information Regulations 2014) that came into force in December 2014 changed the way that information about food allergens is displayed on the packaging of pre-packed foods, and given by food businesses such as early years settings. This law means food businesses like early years settings must be able to indicate to customers (parents and children) which allergens are present in the food and drink they provide. The 14 allergens are: celery, cereals containing gluten (including wheat, rye, barley and oats), crustaceans (including prawns, crab and lobster), eggs, fish, lupin, milk, molluscs (including squid, mussels, cockles, whelks and snails), mustard, nuts, peanuts, sesame seeds, soya beans and sulphur dioxide/sulphites at levels above 10mg/kg.

The recipes in this book have been checked by Children's Food Trust nutritionists, and are labelled to indicate which of the 14 allergens they contain. If a recipe contains any of the listed allergens, the relevant allergen picture will be shown on the top of the page. This information relates to the ingredients listed in the recipe main ingredients list, but it is important to remember that products can be reformulated, and that different brands of products may contain different allergens. Therefore, it is important to check the ingredients and products you are using by reading product labels or by checking with suppliers to ensure you are aware of any allergens contained in food you buy. For more information on how this will affect labelling of food provided by early years settings, visit the Food Standards Agency website. All margarine used within recipes in this booklet is a vegetable fat spread and does not contain milk or dairy products.

Meals and snacks prepared and photographed by Helena Little (Brave Design) and Erica Hocking. Additional photos with kind permission from the Caroline Walker Trust.

Resources and support

Allergy UK
www.allergyuk.org/food-allergy-menu/food-allergy

Children's Food Trust British Food Chart:
www.childrensfoodtrust.org.uk/resources/seasonalitychart

Children's Food Trust Seasonal menus and recipes for early years settings:
www.childrensfoodtrust.org.uk/eatbetterstartbetter/examplemenus

Children's Food Trust Voluntary Food and Drink Guidelines for Earl Years Settings in England:
www.childrensfoodtrust.org.uk/eatbetterstartbetter/practicalguide

EU Food Information for Consumers Regulation (No. 1169/ 2011)
www.ec.europa.eu/food/food/labellingnutrition/foodlabelling/proposed_legislation_en.htm

Food Standards Agency (FSA)
www.food.gov.uk/business-industry/allergy-guide/allergen-resources

Exploring new tastes: savoury main dishes

Recipe 1: Mixed bean and root vegetable stew

SULPHITES

Suggested portion size for recipe

1-4 years: 120g
1-2 years: 100g
3-4 years: 140g

Preparation time: 40 minutes
Cooking time: 40 minutes

Ingredients	Quantity - serves 5	Quantity - serves 20
Tomato and basil sauce		
Onion, peeled	120g (1 medium)	480g (2 large)
Fresh basil	2 tablespoons	4 tablespoons
Garlic, peeled	1 clove	4 cloves
Vegetable oil	1 tablespoon	4 tablespoons
Tomato purée	1 tablespoon	2 tablespoons
Canned tomatoes, chopped	1 x 200g can	1 x 400g can
Stew		
Onion, peeled	60g (1 small)	240g (1 large)
Parsnip, peeled	45g (½ small)	180g (2 medium)
Carrot, peeled	60g (½ medium)	240g (3 medium)
Vegetable oil	½ tablespoon	2 tablespoons
Garlic purée	½ teaspoon	2 teaspoons
Canned kidney beans, no added salt and sugar, drained	½ x 215g can (drained weight, 60g)	1 x 400g can (drained weight, 250g)
Canned haricot beans, no added salt and sugar, drained	½ x 215g can (drained weight, 60g)	½ x 400g can (drained weight, 250g)
Canned butter beans, no added salt and sugar, drained	½ x 215g can (drained weight, 60g)	½ x 400g can (drained weight, 250g)
Water	100ml	400ml

Method

1. Prepare the tomato and basil sauce following the recipe. Heat the oil in a pan, add the onion and garlic and fry for 2–3 minutes. Add the tomato purée, chopped tomatoes and basil to the pan, bring to the boil and simmer for 15 minutes.

2. Now start on the rest of the stew. Chop the onion, parsnip and carrot into 2cm cubes.

3. Heat the oil in a large pan, add the onion and cook for 5 minutes until the onion softens.

4. Add the garlic purée, parsnips, carrot, beans, water and tomato sauce, bring to the boil and leave to simmer for 30–40 minutes until the vegetables are soft.

Serving suggestion: Serve with apricot and herb couscous.

Top tip: If you are short of time, use canned tomatoes or passata and fresh herbs instead of the tomato and basil sauce.

Recipe adapted with permission from: Early Years Catering at Illminster Avenue, Children's Food Trust Autumn/Winter menu and recipes for early years settings, page 25: **www.childrensfoodtrust.org.uk/eatbetterstartbetter/examplemenus**

© Children's Food Trust 2015

STAR
WARS

Recipe 2: Lamb curry

Suggested portion size for recipe

1-4 years: 100g
1-2 years: 85g
3-4 years: 115g

Preparation time: 15 minutes
Cooking time: 40 minutes

Ingredients	Quantity – serves 5	Quantity – serves 20
Onion, peeled	75g (1 small)	300g (2 medium)
Carrot, peeled	30g (1 small)	120g (4 small)
Fresh tomatoes	40g (½ medium)	160g (2 medium)
Vegetable oil	½ tablespoon	2 tablespoons
Lamb, lean, diced	250g	1 kg
Tomato purée	1 tablespoon	4 tablespoons
Ground turmeric	1 teaspoon	4 teaspoons
Curry powder	½ heaped teaspoon	2 heaped teaspoons
Chilli powder	½ teaspoon	2 teaspoons
Water	250ml	1L

Method

1. Chop the onion, carrot and tomatoes.
2. Heat the oil in a pan and add the diced lamb. Cook until browned.
3. Add the onion, carrots and tomatoes and cook for 5 minutes.
4. Add the tomato purée, turmeric, curry powder, chilli powder and water. Bring to the boil and simmer for 30 minutes or until the lamb is cooked and the vegetables are soft.

✔ **Serving suggestion:** Serve with brown rice and tomato and coriander salad.

✱ **Top tip:** Dice the lamb into small chunks to reduce the cooking time.

Recipe adapted with permission from: Eden Foodservice, Children's Food Trust Autumn/Winter menu and recipes for early years settings, page 21:
www.childrensfoodtrust.org.uk/eatbetterstartbetter/examplemenus

© Children's Food Trust 2015

Recipe 3: Beef and vegetable enchiladas

Suggested portion size for recipe

1-4 years: 140g
1-2 years: 120g
3-4 years: 160g

Preparation time: 60 minutes
Cooking time: 30 minutes

Ingredients	Quantity - serves 5	Quantity - serves 20
Onion, peeled	60g (1 small)	240g (1 large)
Fresh red pepper, cored	80g ($\frac{1}{2}$ medium)	320g (2 medium)
Mushrooms	20g (2 mushrooms)	80g (8 mushrooms)
Vegetable oil	$\frac{1}{2}$ tablespoon	2 tablespoons
Canned tomatoes, chopped	200g (1 x 200g can)	800g (2 x 400g cans)
Garlic purée	$\frac{1}{2}$ teaspoon	2 teaspoons
Tomato purée	1 teaspoon	1 heaped tablespoon
Water	50ml	200ml
Dried mixed herbs	$\frac{1}{4}$ teaspoon	1 teaspoon
Frying beef steak	210g	850g
Tortilla wraps	150g (approx. $2\frac{1}{2}$ large wraps)	600g (approx. 10 large wraps)
Cheddar cheese, full-fat	50g	200g

Method

1. Preheat the oven to 220°C/425°F/gas mark 7.

2. Wash and chop the onion, red pepper and mushrooms.

3. Heat the oil in a large pan and add the onions. Cook until softened (approximately 5 minutes).

4. Add the mushrooms and peppers and cook for a further 10 minutes. When cooked remove from the heat and blend the vegetables.

5. Put the blended vegetables back into the pan with the canned tomatoes, garlic purée, tomato purée, water and herbs and simmer on a low heat for 30 minutes.

6. Meanwhile, slice the beef into thin strips and fry in a separate pan until browned. Add to the tomato and vegetable mixture.

7. In an oven proof dish, layer the sauce and tortilla, repeating to the top. Finish with the sauce and sprinkle the cheese on top.

8. Bake in the oven for around 30 minutes until the cheese has melted and turned golden.

✔ **Serving suggestion:** Serve with traditional Mexican dips such as guacamole and sour cream.

✱ **Top tip:** Try with strips of chicken instead of beef.

Recipe adapted with permission from: Busy Bees Nursery, Children's Food Trust Spring/summer menu and recipes for early years settings, page 44: **www.childrensfoodtrust.org.uk/eatbetterstartbetter/examplemenus**

© Children's Food Trust 2015

Recipe 4: Chicken risotto

Suggested portion size for recipe

1-4 years: 170g
1-2 years: 145g
3-4 years: 195g

Preparation time: 15 minutes
Cooking time: 30-40 minutes

Ingredients	Quantity – serves 5	Quantity – serves 20
Onion, peeled	60g (1 small)	240g (1 large)
Garlic, peeled	1 clove	4 cloves
Fresh red pepper, cored	100g (1 small pepper)	400g (4 small)
Vegetable oil	½ tablespoon	2 tablespoons
Chicken breast, diced	200g	800g
White rice	150g	600g
Stock	300ml	1.6L
Frozen peas	50g	200g
Fresh parsley	3 sprigs	12 sprigs

Method

1. Chop the onion, garlic and pepper.
2. Heat the oil in a pan, add the onion and garlic and cook until softened.
3. Add the diced chicken and cook for 10 minutes.
4. Add the peppers and rice and fry for a few minutes.
5. Pour over ¾ of the stock and cook until almost all the water has been absorbed by the rice.
6. Add the frozen peas and gradually add the remaining water until the rice is soft and the risotto is creamy.
7. Chop the parsley and stir into the risotto before serving.

✔ **Serving suggestion:** Serve with grated parmesan.

✱ **Top tip:** Use herbs and spices to add flavour to the water rather than stock.

Recipe adapted with permission from: Sheri Akambi (Childminder), Children's Food Trust Autumn/Winter menu and recipes for early years settings, page 46: **www.childrensfoodtrust.org.uk/eatbetterstartbetter/examplemenus**

© Children's Food Trust 2015

Recipe 5: Fish pie with sweet potato

Suggested portion size for recipe

1-4 years: 170g
1-2 years: 145g
3-4 years: 195g

Preparation time: 45 minutes
Cooking time: 30 minutes

Ingredients	Quantity - serves 5	Quantity - serves 20
Sweet potato, peeled	350g	1.4kg
White, floury potatoes, peeled	100g	400g
Salmon, fresh	80g	320g
Haddock, fresh	80g	320g
Smoked haddock, fresh	50g	200g
Whole milk	250ml	1L
Soft margarine	20g	80g
Plain flour	15g	60g

Method

1. Preheat the oven to 180°C/350°F/gas mark 4.

2. Chop the potato and sweet potato into 2cm cubes. Boil in water for 15 minutes or until soft.

3. Meanwhile put the salmon, haddock and smoked haddock in a large pan, cover with the milk (reserving some for the mashed potato) and simmer for 20 minutes or until the fish is cooked. Remove the fish, check for bones and set aside. Reserve the milk.

4. Drain the potatoes and then mash with enough margarine and milk to make a smooth consistency.

5. Prepare a roux white sauce: melt the remaining margarine in a pan on a low heat. Once the margarine has melted, add the flour and mix well. Gradually add the milk used to poach the fish to the margarine and flour mixture, stirring continuously until the sauce is smooth and thick.

6. Flake the fish into the white sauce, taking care to remove all bones.

7. Pour the fish mixture into a large ovenproof dish and top with the mashed potato.

8. Bake in the oven for 30 minutes or until piping hot throughout.

✔ **Serving suggestion:** Serve with swede and cauliflower.

✱ **Top tip:** Add chopped fresh herbs to the white sauce to add colour and flavour.

Recipe adapted with permission from: Acorn Grove Nursery, Children's Food Trust Autumn/Winter menu and recipes for early years settings, page 23: **www.childrensfoodtrust.org.uk/eatbetterstartbetter/examplemenus**

© Children's Food Trust 2015

Catering for all children: vegetarian main dishes

Recipe 6: Potato and lentil cakes

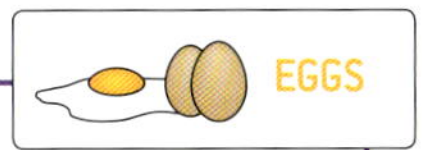

Suggested portion size for recipe

1-4 years: 130g
1-2 years: 105g
3-4 years: 150g

Preparation time: 55 minutes
Cooking time: 30 minutes

Ingredients	Quantity - serves 5	Quantity - serves 20
Vegetable oil	1 tablespoon	4 tablespoons
Baking potatoes, peeled	400g ($2\frac{1}{2}$ medium)	1.6kg (10 large)
Onion, peeled	60g (1 small)	240g (1 large)
Green lentils	20g	80g
Red lentils	30g	120g
Mixed herbs, dried	1 teaspoon	4 teaspoons
Wholemeal bread	50g	200g
	(2 medium slices)	(10 medium slices)
Egg	50g (1 egg)	100g (2 eggs)

Method

1. Preheat the oven to 200°C /400°F/gas mark 6. Grease a baking tray with half the oil.
2. Chop the potatoes and onions. Put the potatoes in a pan, cover with water and boil for 20 minutes or until soft
3. In a separate pan of boiling water add the green lentils and boil for 10 minutes. After 10 minutes add the red lentils and boil for a further 20 minutes before draining.
4. Drain the potatoes and mash them until smooth.
5. Heat half the oil in a frying pan, add the onion and fry for 5 minutes or until soft.
6. Combine the potatoes, onions, lentils and herbs in a large bowl.
7. Make the bread into breadcrumbs and beat the egg in a bowl.
8. Roll the potato and lentil mixture into balls, coat in egg and breadcrumbs and place on the greased baking tray.
9. Bake in the oven for 20-30 minutes.

✔ **Serving suggestion:** Serve with tomato relish.

✱ **Top tip:** Use fresh herbs to add colour and flavour.

Recipe adapted with permission from: Acorn Grove Nursery, Children's Food Trust Autumn/Winter menu and recipes for early years settings, page 51: **www.childrensfoodtrust.org.uk/eatbetterstartbetter/examplemenus**

© Children's Food Trust 2015

Recipe 7: Chickpea and vegetable curry

Suggested portion size for recipe

1-4 years: 120g
1-2 years: 110g
3-4 years: 130g

Preparation time: 20 minutes
Cooking time: 45 minutes

Ingredients	Quantity – serves 5	Quantity – serves 20
Onion, peeled	60g (1 small)	240g (1 large)
Garlic, peeled	½ clove	2 cloves
Vegetable oil	½ tablespoon	2 tablespoons
Flour, plain	15g (1 tablespoon)	60g (4 tablespoons)
Curry powder	½ tablespoon	2 tablespoons
Cumin, ground	½ teaspoon	2 teaspoons
Coriander, ground	½ teaspoon	2 teaspoons
Tomato purée	½ tablespoon	2 tablespoons
Water	300ml	1.2L
Desiccated coconut	7g (½ tablespoon)	30g (2 tablespoons)
Canned chickpeas,	¾ x 400g can	3 x 400g cans
no added salt or sugar, drained	(drained weight, 175g)	(drained weight, 700g)
Vegetables, mixed frozen	150g	600g

Method

1. Chop the onion and garlic.
2. Heat the oil in a large pan, add the onion and garlic and cook until soft.
3. Stir in the flour, curry powder, cumin, coriander and tomato purée. Mix until blended into a paste.
4. Gradually stir the water into the mixture, until the desired consistency is achieved.
5. Add the coconut, chickpeas and vegetables and simmer for approximately 45 minutes.

✔ **Serving suggestion:** Serve with brown rice.

✱ **Top tip:** Try with fresh seasonal vegetables.

Recipe adapted with permission from: The Field's Children Centre, Children's Food Trust Spring/Summer menu and recipes for early years settings, page 26: **www.childrensfoodtrust.org.uk/eatbetterstartbetter/examplemenus**

© Children's Food Trust 2015

Recipe 8: Quorn™ and vegetable couscous

EGGS

CEREALS CONTAINING GLUTEN

Suggested portion size for recipe

1-4 years: 150g
1-2 years: 130g
3-4 years: 170g

Preparation time: 10 minutes plus chilling time
Cooking time: None

Ingredients	Quantity – serves 5	Quantity – serves 20
Couscous	180g	720g
Water	225ml	900ml
Quorn™ pieces, cooked	175g	700g
Fresh peppers, cored	60g (½ small)	240g (1½ medium)
Fresh tomato	85g (1 medium)	340g (4 medium)
Fresh coriander	½ teaspoon	2 teaspoons
Fresh parsley	½ teaspoon	2 teaspoons
Cucumber	60g	240g
Olive oil	½ tablespoon	2 tablespoons

Method

1. Boil the water and pour over the couscous in a bowl. Cover with cling film and leave to stand for 5 minutes or until all the water has been absorbed.

2. Meanwhile, chop the remaining ingredients.

3. When the couscous is ready, fluff with a fork and stir in the chopped Quorn™, vegetables, herbs and olive oil. Chill and serve.

✔ **Serving suggestion:** Serve with vegetable sticks.

✱ **Top tip:** This recipe can be prepared and stored in advance.

Recipe adapted with permission from: Caroline Walker Trust, Children's Food Trust Spring/Summer menu and recipes for early years settings, page 49:
www.childrensfoodtrust.org.uk/eatbetterstartbetter/examplemenus

© Children's Food Trust 2015

Recipe 9: Savoury omelette

EGGS

Suggested portion size for recipe

1-4 years: 70g
1-2 years: 60g
3-4 years: 80g

Preparation time: 20 minutes
Cooking time: 15 minutes

Ingredients	Quantity - serves 5	Quantity - serves 20
New potato	50g (1)	200g (4)
Onion, peeled	30g (½ small)	120g (2 small)
Fresh mixed peppers, cored	30g	120g
Eggs	250g (5 eggs)	1kg (20 eggs)
Vegetable oil	½ tablespoon	2 tablespoons

Method

1. Wash and chop the potato, onion and pepper. Boil the potato in unsalted water until cooked. (Approximately 10 minutes.)
2. Drain the water from the potato and leave to cool, then dice.
3. Crack the eggs into a mixing bowl and beat.
4. Heat the oil in a frying pan and add the onions and peppers. Cook until soft.
5. Add the diced, cooled potato and pour the egg over the ingredients.
6. Cook until the eggs are set and the base is golden then finish cooking under the grill.

Serving suggestion: Serve with potato salad and cucumber.

Top tip: Preheat the grill to help cook the top of the omelette at the end.

Recipe adapted with permission from: Caroline Walker Trust, Children's Food Trust Spring/Summer menu and recipes for early years settings, page 51: **www.childrensfoodtrust.org.uk/eatbetterstartbetter/examplemenus**

© Children's Food Trust 2015

Recipe 10: Ratatouille and mozzarella

Suggested portion size for recipe

1-4 years: 50g ratatouille and 15g mozzarella
1-2 years: 40g ratatouille and 15g mozzarella
3-4 years: 60g ratatouille and 15g mozzarella

Preparation time: 10 minutes
Cooking time: 30 minutes

Ingredients	Quantity - serves 5	Quantity - serves 20
Onion, peeled	30g (½ small)	120g (2 small)
Garlic, peeled	½ clove	2 cloves
Mushrooms	30g (3 mushrooms)	120g (12 mushrooms)
Courgette	50g (½ medium)	200g (2 medium)
Canned tomatoes, chopped	200g (1 x 200g can)	800g (2 x 400g cans)
Dried oregano	¼ teaspoon	1 teaspoon
Dried thyme	¼ teaspoon	1 teaspoon
Water	50ml	200ml
Mozzarella	75g	300g

Method

1. Chop the onion, garlic, mushrooms and courgette.

2. Put the onion, garlic, mushrooms, courgettes, canned tomatoes, oregano, thyme and water into a large saucepan, bring to the boil and then simmer until all the vegetables are cooked (approximately 30 minutes).

3. Grate the mozzarella, and serve with the ratatouille.

Serving suggestion: Serve with a jacket potato.

Top tip: Try with crumbled feta cheese instead of mozzarella.

Recipe adapted with permission from: Pollyanna's Nursery, Children's Food Trust Spring/summer menu and recipes for early years settings, page 50: **www.childrensfoodtrust.org.uk/eatbetterstartbetter/examplemenus**

© Children's Food Trust 2015

Well balanced treats: puddings

Recipe 11: Raspberry purée and fromage frais

Suggested portion size for recipe

1-4 years: 100g (60g fromage frais, and 40g purée)
1-2 years: 90g (50g fromage frais, and 40g purée)
3-4 years: 110g (70g fromage frais, and 40g purée)

Preparation time: 5 minutes
Cooking time: None

Ingredients	Quantity - serves 5	Quantity - serves 20
Raspberries, fresh	200g	800g
Plain fromage frais, full-fat	300g	1.2kg

Method

1. Wash the raspberries.

2. Add the raspberries to a food processor and blend until smooth.

3. Serve the puréed raspberries on top of the fromage frais.

Serving suggestion: Mix the purée into the yoghurt to make a ripple effect.

Top tip: Try with peaches.

Recipe adapted with permission from: Old School House Day Nursery, Children's Food Trust Spring/Summer menu and recipes for early years settings page 40: **www.childrensfoodtrust.org.uk/eatbetterstartbetter/examplemenus**

© Children's Food Trust 2015

Recipe 12: Cocoa and beetroot cake

EGGS

CEREALS CONTAINING GLUTEN

Suggested portion size for recipe

1-4 years: 50g
1-2 years: 40g
3-4 years: 60g

Preparation time: 15 minutes
Cooking time: 30 minutes

Ingredients	Quantity - serves 10	Quantity - serves 20
Beetroot , raw, peeled	65g	130g
Cocoa powder	35g (1½ tablespoons)	70g (3 tablespoons)
Wholemeal flour	100g	200g
Baking powder	1½ teaspoons	3 teaspoons
Bicarbonate of soda	½ teaspoon	1 teaspoon
Vegetable oil	60ml	120ml
Caster sugar	100g	200g
Egg	100g (2 medium)	200g (4 medium)

Method

1. Preheat the oven to 200°C /400°F/gas mark 6. Grease and line a cake tin.
2. Wash and grate the beetroot.
3. Mix the cocoa, flour, baking powder, bicarbonate of soda, oil, caster sugar and egg in a large bowl and beat until smooth and light in colour
4. Stir in the beetroot.
5. Pour into the cake tin and bake in the oven for approximately 30 minutes.

Serving suggestion: Serve with cocoa custard.

Top tip: Make into muffins.

Recipe adapted with permission from: Eden Foodservice, Children's Food Trust Autumn/Winter menu and recipes for early years settings, page 37: **www.childrensfoodtrust.org.uk/eatbetterstartbetter/examplemenus**

© Children's Food Trust 2015

Recipe 13: Warm winter salad

Suggested portion size for recipe

1-4 years: 40g
1-2 years: 40g
3-4 years: 40g

Preparation time: 10 minutes
Cooking time: 10 minutes

Ingredients	Quantity - serves 5	Quantity - serves 20
Fresh pear, peeled	80g (½ medium)	320g (½ medium)
Fresh orange, peeled	80g (½ medium)	320g (½ medium)
Cranberry juice	50ml	200ml
Ground cinnamon	1 teaspoon	4 teaspoons

Method

1. Core the pear and break the orange into segments. Chop the fruit.

2. Warm the fruit, juice and cinnamon in a large pan on a low heat until the fruit has softened.

✔ **Serving suggestion:** Serve with vanilla sauce.

✱ **Top tip:** Use different seasonal fruits each month. For more information, see the Children's Food Trust British Food Chart in Resources, pages XX.

Recipe adapted with permission from: Busy Bees Nursery, Children's Food Trust Autumn/Winter menu and recipes for early years settings, page 42: **www.childrensfoodtrust.org.uk/eatbetterstartbetter/examplemenus**

© Children's Food Trust 2015

Recipe 14: Banana cinnamon rice pudding

Suggested portion size for recipe

1-4 years: 120g
1-2 years: 100g
3-4 years: 140g

Preparation time: 10 minutes
Cooking time: 2 hours

Ingredients	Quantity - serves 10	Quantity - serves 20
Pudding rice	75g	150g
Caster sugar	30g (1½ tablespoons)	60g (3 tablespoons)
Whole milk	600ml	1.2L
Banana	400g (4)	800g (8)
Cinnamon	1 teaspoon	2 teaspoons

Method

1. Preheat the oven to 160°C/325°F/gas mark 3 and grease an ovenproof dish.
2. Wash the rice in a sieve and put it in the dish with the sugar.
3. Heat the milk in a pan and pour over the rice and sugar.
4. Bake in the oven for 1½-2 hours until the rice is tender.
5. Place the bananas in their skins on a baking tray and bake in the oven for 30 minutes.
6. After 30 minutes, remove the bananas from the oven, scoop out the banana flesh from the skins. Blend the banana flesh and cinnamon to a smooth purée. Combine with the rice pudding or serve separately.

Serving suggestion: Use stewed apples instead of bananas.

Top tip: Take care when removing the hot banana flesh from the skins.

Recipe adapted with permission from: Marsha Mclarty (Childminder) and Eden Foodservice, Children's Food Trust Autumn/Winter menu and recipes for early years settings, page 58: **www.childrensfoodtrust.org.uk/eatbetterstartbetter/examplemenus**

© Children's Food Trust 2015

Recipe 15: Crunchy summer crumble and yoghurt

Suggested portion size for recipe

1-4 years: 120g (60g crumble, and 60g yoghurt)
1-2 years: 100g (50g crumble, and 50g yoghurt)
3-4 years: 140g (70g crumble, and 70g yoghurt)

Preparation time: 20 minutes
Cooking time: 35 minutes

Ingredients	Quantity - serves 10	Quantity - serves 20
Cooking apples, peeled and cored	300g	600g
Fresh raspberries	100g	200g
Soft margarine	40g	80g
Plain flour	50g	100g
Wholemeal flour	30g	60g
Caster sugar	40g	80g
Cornflakes	50g	100g
Plain yoghurt (full fat)	600g	1.2kg

Method

1. Preheat the oven to 190°C/375°F/gas mark 5.

2. Slice the apples and place in the bottom of an ovenproof dish. Wash and scatter the raspberries over the apples and mix gently.

3. Gently rub together the margarine and flour until it resembles fine breadcrumbs. Add the sugar and cornflakes and combine, but do not over mix.

4. Sprinkle the crumble mixture evenly over the fruit and bake in the oven for 30-35 minutes. Serve with plain yoghurt.

✓ **Serving suggestion:** Replace the yoghurt with custard.

✱ **Top tip:** Try with different combinations of fruit. Frozen fruit is great for crumbles.

Recipe adapted with permission from: Eden Foodservice, Children's Food Trust Spring/summer menu and recipes for early years settings, page 57: **www.childrensfoodtrust.org.uk/eatbetterstartbetter/examplemenus**
© Children's Food Trust 2015

PACEY resources

We offer our members a range of opportunities in childcare training, qualifications and knowledge

- Exclusive, free high-quality online training across childcare subjects
- Exclusive pricing on PACEY qualifications and training
- Exclusive member discounts on essential items in the PACEY shop
- PACEY webinars (online interactive workshops) – learn from the comfort of your own home
- Opportunities to take part in childcare research
- Up to date information on the latest childcare topics and debates via our email alerts and forums
- Freelance opportunities for experienced childcare experts.

We have fun ways to stay up to date, evidence your framework and keep your professional development going strong

- Easy-access practice videos
- Simple and clear childcare factsheets
- In-depth practice guides
- Monthly e-newsletters on the sector, policy and events
- Monthly practice bulletins on things you need to know
- Free downloadable children's resources
- Childcare Professional magazine delivered to your door
- Free Childcare helpline – speak to a PACEY expert for help on any childcare subject
- Free Legal and Wellbeing support lines – for your personal and family use

Professional Standards

The PACEY Professional Standards are based on the competencies, knowledge, skills and behaviours that an early years and childcare professional requires every day to carry out the key role they play in the lives of the children and families they work with. The Professional Standards support members in:

- Reflecting on all areas of your practice
- Identifying your individual professional development
- Identifying your individual needs
- Continually extending and improving your practice

The Standards are separated into four areas:

Children First – This area focuses on child development; valuing each child's individual needs and differences whilst empowering them to reach their full potential; safeguarding; and transitions.

Enabling Environments – Is about ensuring you have a safe and welcoming setting; working in partnership with and supporting parents and carers; and making the most of local services and facilities.

My Professional Role – Covers the importance of reflective practice; balancing your work and career with your personal commitments; and evaluating and improving the quality of your practice.

Childcare Service – Is concerned with meeting the relevant laws, regulations and benchmarks for quality; and also running a childcare business.

These four areas form the basis for PACEY's Professional Standards and we have developed membership categories through which members can progress. For more information, visit **www.pacey.org.uk/professional**

Access groups and benefits to support you every step of the way

- Be part of the professional childcare community and enjoy the strength of a large peer network
- Help shape policy and ensure your voice is heard through PACEY's influence at Government level
- Take part online and at a local level through PACEY Local
- Show parents and Ofsted (in England) or CSSIW (in Wales) your commitment and professionalism through professional membership
- Show your PACEY membership on your business cards and marketing materials
- Use the free vacancy matching service to increase your business (childminders only)

pacey | Local

Peer support

PACEY Local is our peer-to-peer support and online community network for early years and childcare professionals. As well as an online community, PACEY Local offers face-to-face meetings across England and Wales.

The local groups offer an opportunity to meet socially with other childcare professionals; to help each other with planning; or to attend drop-in sessions and local trips out with the children you care for.

The PACEY Local online community is another way to get involved, allowing you to connect with childcare professionals across England and Wales.

To find your local group, visit **local.pacey.org.uk**

Find out more

If you are already a member of PACEY, **visit www.pacey. org.uk** and log into MyPACEY to find out more about the range of resources available to you. If you're not already a member, visit **www.pacey.org.uk/join**

Further reading

Children's Food Trust British Seasonal Food Chart: **www.childrensfoodtrust.org.uk/assets/rsrcs/british-seasonal-food-charts/cft_sfdchart_a1final.pdf**

Early Years Outcomes (England): **www.foundationyears.org.uk**

The Food Safety Handbook (Level 2) – Springer R (2009)
Statutory Framework for the Early Years Foundation Stage (England): **www.foundationyears.org.uk**

Food and Health Guidelines (Wales): **gov.wales/topics/health/improvement/index/guidelines/?lang=en**

Food Standards Agency: **www.food.gov.uk**

Framework for Children's Learning for 3- to 7-year-olds in Wales: **gov.wales/docs/dcells/publications/141111-framework-for-childrens-learning-for-3-to-7-year-olds-en.pdf**

National Minimum Standards for Regulated Childcare (Wales): **cssiw.org.uk/docs/cssiw/publications/120309regchildcareen.pdf**

PACEY – Food Hygiene Factsheets and training course: **www.pacey.org.uk/mypacey**

Reckitt Benckiser (2010) *Keep it clean and healthy* 4th Edition. Pat Cole, Cambridgeshire

Safer Food Better Business for Caterers – for childcares working in a group setting: **www.food.gov.uk/business-industry/caterers/sfbb**

Safer Food Better Business for Childminders: **www.food.gov.uk/business-industry/caterers/sfbb**